GREAT WES

Reflections

DEDICATION

To David, my son and most ardent fan.

GREAT WESTERN

T. H. Terry

Oxford Publishing Co.

Typesetting by:
Aquarius Typesetting Services, New Milton, Hants.

Printed in Great Britain by:
Hollen Street Press Ltd, Slough, Berks.

Published by:
Oxford Publishing Co.
Link House
West Street
POOLE, Dorset

ACKNOWLEDGEMENTS

I am indebted to many good people who have provided material for this book, including C. R. L. Rice, Esq., ex-Chief Running & Maintenance Officer of the Midland Division of the LMR for his kindness and encouragement, and Howard Jones, Esq., J.P, ex-GWR driver, whose friendship and co-operation in railway matters I look back on with extreme pleasure. Thanks are also due to W. C. Stride, ex-engineman, for his efforts on my behalf, and to my daughter, Pat, and my daughter-in-law, Avril, for their extreme kindness and patience in typing the script from my very poor handwriting and a surfeit of hieroglyphics. My thanks are also given to Revd. Alan Knight, Vicar of the Church of the Holy Cross, Mark, for his kindness in reading the manuscript.

Contents

FOREWORD

Many pens far abler than mine have set down the history of the one time Great Western Railway, and it would be extremely presumptuous on my part to even try to emulate their very excellent tomes. It is the desire of the writer to present his 'own personal experiences' of a lifetime's association with an organisation he held in the highest regard — the Great Western Railway.

I have been an ardent admirer for many years of those gentlemen responsible for the monumental works which have so ably portrayed the progress of the Great Western Railway from earliest times, and their extremely well tabulated tables of the performances of steam locomotives and the designers.

Well-earned tributes have been paid to the excellence of design which rendered these performances possible, and many eulogies have been expressed in this way to gentlemen of whom I have many recollections in the field of locomotive design, including Churchward, Hall and Stanier. Also, of course, many excellent works have been written regarding that 'giant' of railway architecture, Isambard Kingdom Brunel, for whom all Great Western men, in my day, had a deep and abiding respect.

I therefore leave all these greater issues to men far abler than I, and will endeavour to confine myself to the business of life as I, a footplateman, saw it during the major part of fifty years on the Great Western Railway. Although steam locomotion is now only a shadow of its former self, the balance of intense interest is possibly greater at this time than existed when steam was at its zenith, and it is with intense satisfaction and extreme pleasure in the knowledge that literally thousands of enthusiasts, very many of whom were too young to appreciate the sight and sound of a steam locomotive, are now numbered in clubs and associations all over the British Isles and, indeed, in many countries abroad.

CHAPTER ONE

My Debut with the 'Western'

My story begins as a young boy at school, with the usual hankering at that time to become an engine driver. In my childish imagination, I envisaged the engine driver living with a sort of halo around his head, and all he had to was to sit in his cab admiring the scenery as his great steed thundered along the track.

How wrong I was and, of course, little did I know the many vicissitudes I should encounter before assuming such an august role, and realise the responsibility of working these engines of such potential power and speed. Due to events which I shall explain later, it was to be 23 years before I eventually reached my ultimate goal.

I entered the service of the Great Western Railway on 18th November 1919, and very soon discovered, for various reasons to be described later, that railway service was not exactly a bed of roses. The Great Western Railway was, in my opinion, an organisation second to none in the field of railway service; this included good timekeeping, safety, overall efficiency and, above all, a meticulous discipline throughout its ranks — from the highest to the most junior position.

There was a slogan in those days which I well remember, many times to my cost — 'Only the best is good enough for the Great Western Railway'. Although the implication was, at times, somewhat trying, in various circumstances, it certainly produced results, and was a means of welding together, if that is the correct term, a wonderful body full of 'esprit de corps' who operated not by pressure, in the main, but because they were 'Western' with a tradition to uphold; a tradition left by that great railway builder Isambard Kingdom Brunel, and the men who followed him.

I was engaged as an engine cleaner, and was employed in that capacity for the next five years, during which time the acquisition of some knowledge of the ultimate duties of fireman was expected. The staff were also very forcibly reminded of the necessity for good timekeeping, and I found the experience of signing on at 5a.m. rather trying, in view of the fact that at that time I lived some considerable distance from the locomotive shed, and was only vaguely aware that such a time existed!

Any deviation from the rules was quickly dealt with 'on the mat'; a rather terrifying experience to us, with the possible consequences of any repetition necessitating a visit to the 'beak'. It was always with the greatest trepidation that we knocked on his door, cap in hand,

and waited for the summons to enter, which was usually given in a manner that dissipated what little courage we had. I well remember Williams, our Locomotive Depot Chief, a man who had risen from the ranks and knew all the answers, a person with the task of running the very large shed with its very many and varied responsibilities. He in turn was answerable to a higher authority for any irregularities occurring locally, and was something of a martinet, but he also possessed many kindly human attributes which surfaced from time to time. For persistant recalcitrants he had no time, and they were quickly disposed of. Such was the set-up; a more or less rigid discipline which we came to accept and, of course, with so many young men present, there was always the occasion when youthful exuberance merited the visit to the chief 'down the passage'. Many of these interviews with the 'beak' were the result of an extremely meticulous foreman cleaner, a very just and forthright man, who would brook no deviation from the general code of conduct and, bearing in mind my previous remarks concerning a crowd of boys of all sorts of character, he had quite a difficult time keeping us all on the straight and narrow. Through him we learned a philosophy which was to remain with us and, indeed, stood us in good stead throughout our railway careers.

We cleaners were a motley crew. In the main, the majority were young men from what we termed 'foreign stations'; boys who were unable to obtain employment at the smaller locomotive depots of their native place, and had, perforce, to come to Tyseley, Birmingham, if they wished to enter railway service. Thus, in these cases, amidst a variety of pseudonyms, they were given the name of their place of origin, which sometimes remained with them long after they had left the cleaning stage, and had been promoted to firemen and, in some extreme cases, even after they had become enginemen.

Not all, of course, were named after their place of origin, as many were named according to some trait or alleged peculiarity, although it was a source of wonder to me why certain individuals should answer to Rubberneck, Bladder, Donkey, Hot Box, and Seventy Break; the latter possibly being given due to his alleged prowess at the game of billiards. Also among the many Toms, Dicks and Harrys there were the names of White or Miller which invariably assumed the verbal appendage of Snowy and Dusty respectively. We also had a Clark, but why this particular name should be construed as 'Knobby' has always escaped me.

Tyseley Locomotive Shed was one of the larger depots on the GWR system, employing several hundred drivers, firemen and shed staff, including eighty cleaners. There was something of the order of 100 steam locomotives of varying size, from the smallest shunting engine to the largest passenger locomotive then in use. The latter were magnificent machines, with names such as *Rob Roy*, a really beautiful example of her particular class, and great numbers were built in the early years of the present century. She was a 4-6-0 with coupled wheels of 6ft. 8½in. diameter, a wonderful performer, a stable rider and, invariably, a good steamer in the right hands. In my opinion, one of the finest locomotives ever turned out at Swindon Works. Many of these beautiful engines were named after the stories of Sir Walter Scott; *Red Gauntlet, Ivanhoe, Lady of Shallot* and many others, including the aforementioned *Rob Roy*.

I recall my enthusiasm, whilst still a schoolboy, for a particular display in the window of a tobacconist's shop near my home, which advertised a well-known brand of pipe tobacco and displayed, in all her beautiful livery and lining, No. 2908 *Lady of Quality*. In later life I had the privilege of seeing this particular locomotive, and on each occasion I was very forcibly reminded of my schoolboy aspirations to become an engine driver, and possibly to assume charge of my idol, No. 2908 *Lady of Quality*.

At Tyseley we also had the 'Flower' class locomotives, which were very fine passenger engines with a great turn of speed. These engines had such names as *Marigold, Lobelia, Stephanotis* and *Calceolaria*. Double-framed engines, with wheels of 6ft. 8½in. in a 4-6-0 formation, they were very excellent engines in their day. In the same mould we had 'Atbara' class No. 4120 and 'Armstrong' class No. 7. We also had the 'Bulldog' class with No. 3308 *Falmouth*, a rather smaller edition of the 'Atbara' class, No. 3404 *A. H. Mills*, and No. 3362 *Albert Brassey*, all capable of fast passenger work for which they were designed. The 'Devons' or 'Duke' class, including *Katerfelto, Tre Pol and Pen* and *Mendip* are names that I well recall. Even today, in my early seventies, I still thrill at the sight and sound of a steam locomotive.

Also housed at Tyeseley were several 43XX class locomotives capable of practically any type of work, but requiring expert firing. This particular class, of which several hundred were built, was an all-round utility locomotive, and my contemporaries will possibly recall the 83XX class of this series which had the front end weighted with a very large block of metal, to which the front buffers were attached.

However, at that time, we also had a few 'Aberdares', a 2-6-0 with steam reversing. In connection with this method I remember the many occasions when one of them was being stabled, and was possibly low in steam, a pinch bar had to be employed under the weigh shaft bar shaft to reverse and get the correct balance on the turntable as, of course, the engine had to be properly balanced before the turntable could be moved. We also had two large freight engines, Nos. 2873 and 2875 and, with their massive boilers and straightforward lines, they were always a delight to clean.

Around 1919, a completely new type of engine appeared. These were the 47XX class, of which only nine were built; they had a very large boiler and a rather high wheel and tractive effort, and at times were employed on express passenger work, but due to the boiler being pitched rather higher than usual, a rolling motion was produced at speed, which could be most disconcerting. Due to this, they were removed from passenger working but came into their own in later years on fast freight workings, and this will be outlined in a subsequent chapter.

Some very fine locomotives were to be seen in the not too distant future, and in 1923 came *Caerphilly Castle*, built to the design of our Chief Mechanical Engineer, C. B. Collett. It was the first of a long line of 'Castles' which gave yeoman service and, in the case of the original, ran 1,910,630 miles before being withdrawn in May 1960. An equally famous breed was yet to come, and in 1927 the first of the new 'King' class was built.

In preparation for the new 'King' class, the nameplates were taken off those engines which carried names of monarchs. The original four cylinder engines stabled at Stafford Road, Wolverhampton (and elsewhere), were given, in exchange, the titles of Italian monarchs, and those of the various crowned heads of Europe. Some years later, Tyseley was allocated the locomotives *Queen Matilda* and *Princess Eugenie*.

The 'Hall' class of locomotive was to come, chief amongst which was *Saint Martin*, a remodelled version of the 29XX series, and renumbered 4900, but retaining the name. Nearly 400 of these very remarkable locomotives were built, being 'maids of all work' and capable, with a smaller wheel than the original 29XX 'Saint' class, of performing with any class of train, be it passenger, freight or mineral. At a later stage in the story I shall return to this subject.

The successful working of a steam locomotive called for the closest liaison between driver and fireman. Team working was essential for the well-being of both, and certainly made for better working all round.

During my long association with the shovel, I was fortunate in the drivers I was called upon to work with. It must be remembered that we were sometimes thrown together for five to six years and, of course, acquired a knowledge of the other's likes and dislikes. Some were fastidious, hating the tiniest bit of dust or untidiness in any way, and believe me, it was sometimes extremely difficult to keep the dust down.

A locomotive boiler, steaming well, manifests unmistakable indications apart from the evidence of the pressure gauge. The immediate discolouration of the exhaust, showing that combustion is at once apparent, and also when exhaust is beaten down when passing under bridges, gives an odour which can always be associated with a fire eager for more fuel. The drill then is little and often, feeding the great incandescent mass at regular intervals, depending, of course, on the load and road.

A good fireman 'watching points', keeping the pressure well up when required, and under control when the regulator was closed, was an invaluable asset to his mate, the driver. They made a good team, each aware of the other's capabilities and, naturally, this built up a good spirit, so essential to the safe and proper working of a train, especially a fast and heavy train, when the driver had to devote the major part of his time to the correct running of the train in all sorts of conditions and weather. The provision of a really good fireman relieved him of the necessity of keeping an eye on his mate, with the knowledge that the job was in the right hands.

Keeping one's balance on a swaying footplate was a feat only acquired after long practice. A locomotive at speed can assume really alarming conditions to the uninitiated, and even the most experienced of us had to hold on tightly along certain sections of the road, when the engine could always be expected to give an 'outsize' in kicks and lurches.

You can imagine my feelings when, as a very young and inexperienced fireman I was detailed to work an express train; the regular fireman having gone sick. Several times during the trip I missed the fire hole door completely due to the oscillation of the engine and, on more than one occasion, I put a shovelful of coal over the driver's feet instead of in the firebox. His observations concerning my gymnastics were very interesting, caustic and lurid, and would not bear repetition here! I was very thankful when we eventually arrived back on shed, to see that I was not booked with him next day, as he probably advised the management that he would like a fireman!

In later life, I have met people who have experienced the same emotion when viewing a fast train running past and, indeed, only a few months ago, after speaking of my life on the railway, a gentleman told me of his daily trip to a certain bridge just outside Taunton, from which he would watch the passage of 'The Cornishman' and observe, with awe and trepidation, the motion of the locomotive at a certain point. I may add that although locomotivemen were used to

11

this sort of ride, it would not be the first time that I had been almost thrown off balance, and sometimes I received the odd bruise; in short it was not exactly a motor car ride. Nevertheless, there was always the thrill of a locomotive at speed, and the rhythm of passing over joints at speed produced an elation I can still conjure up, even after such a passage of time.

Diesel locomotives, of course, have the edge on steam and are extremely efficient machines, but they lack the visual impact of a steam locomotive, with its rapidly rotating rods and valve gear, and the exhaust from the chimney giving an indication of the speed and power of the engine in its passage along the track!

An indication of the standard of conduct demanded at the time is illustrated by a personal experience. It was embodied in the rules and regulations of the Great Western Railway that, at the discretion of the Depot Master or Shed Foreman, any driver or fireman could be taken from his rostered turn two hours either way. This was considered necessary to cope with the continually changing conditions respecting the running of special trains, accidents, or anything demanding the alteration of a man's rostered turn of duty.

My proper turn was a Swan Village coal train, booking on duty at 5.20a.m.; office hours in comparison to the usual times we had to contend with, and a nice little day job. Imagine my surprise and dismay when, at 2.30a.m., the call boy was knocking at the door with an order to book within the hour for a Swindon special and, to cap it all, it was a 'double home'. Before I could properly recover my scattered wits, and still half awake, I shouted down that I was refusing the order. Vic, the call boy, scenting trouble, was away like a long dog, and left me wondering what my action would entail. There was nothing much in the house with which to pack a 'double home' box, and this was apart from the disturbance of being away from home.

Vic was back in a few minutes and stated that I was suspended forthwith, and that I was to report to the Depot Master at 9a.m. that same morning; my wife and I were now fully awake to the enormous possibilities and penalties that my action would evoke. I was also extremely angry at the unreasonable attitude of the foreman, although, at the same time, I realised that I was a victim of the system, with all sorts of consequences. There was just the possibility of appealing to the foreman on duty, so after a hurried cup of tea and felicitations from my wife, in a state of mental stress and with practically nothing to take with me, I hastened down to the shed.

On arriving at the time office, I was informed that a spare fireman had been obtained and was preparing the engine, and that my
12

previous orders to report to the Shed Master were still to be obeyed and, in effect, I was virtually suspended. The night foreman was also missing, apparently going on his usual rounds about the shed. After an agonising search I found him on the passenger side and, in spite of protestations that I was willing to go on the job, he refused my request stating 'that anyone who sent an ultimatum of this nature must face the consequences', but, after pleading with him and almost going down on my knees, he finally relented and allowed me to go on the job.

The fireman who was preparing the engine was greatly relieved when I stepped on to the footplate, as it had possibly meant long hours, as he would have had to have been relieved en route to Swindon. So instead of my own turn, a comfortable little job, I found myself in Swindon with almost nothing to eat and very little of the wherewithal to obtain any food, it being the middle of the week and pay day 'far off'; there it was, their's is not to reason why, just try to soldier on like a good worker, or else!

As a sequel to all this, I was to see the time when, in a more favourable position, as temporary Superisor, and assisting this selfsame gentleman on night duty, during the war, I was able to remind him of the events of fifteen years previously. His remarks took the form of 'Harry, we were both employed by the Great Western and, as such, were bound by it's standards'.

Poor Tom, known to us all as 'Wingy', having lost an arm as an engineman many years previously, and I, in my capacity as Supervisor, shared very many vicissitudes relative to the running of the shed during the darker days of the war, when everything was diametrically opposed to the usual running of the depot. Constant demands from control for this and that, with the slow movement of getting engines through the 'run', was regularly the cause of engine crews taking locomotives off the shed with dirty fires and little coal, with a word of encouragement to 'do their best'. In addition, at this time, we had to contend with an entirely new element, an apathy and general disinclination from many firemen to report for duty. In the main, in justice to these men, they had been directed to work on the railways under the 'Essential Works Order', and their hearts were not in the work. Consequently, we were continually faced with providing men, where possible, to man engines booked off the shed throughout the night, and it can be rightly assumed, that our work was not improved by the almost nightly visits or warnings of enemy aircraft, and the necessity for keeping light down to a minimum. This last item, of course, precluded any attempt to clean fires at night, with the result that men took engines off the shed and did their best. However, I am over-running my story.

Where are all my good friends and contemporaries of yesteryear? Many have crossed 'the great divide', but there are still men who, no doubt, remember Tyseley Shed in its heyday. It was a hive of activity, with local services which were many and intensive, local goods, express goods and an express passenger service to many points on the GWR system.

We cleaners were never out of work as we were, in fact, a workforce that could be drawn on for a variety of jobs. The servicing of a locomotive called for a great number and variety of tasks to be performed, including fire dropping, an extremely arduous task, lighting up, tube cleaning and preparing sand for sand-boxes; these were some of the tasks we were called upon to perform during the enforced absence of the regular staff.

The most exciting job was, of course, spare firing, and there was always the anxious perusal of the roster sheets for any spare firing duties the next day, although these were always allocated on a seniority basis. I remember the first time I was booked out, and despite the fact that it was only a shunting engine, it was a start. So my five years of engine cleaning rolled slowly by. We had our moments of course. Jack, a particular lifelong friend, who shared more than just a passing interest in steam locomotives and, even at this very early stage, showed a remarkabe insight into the mechanics of steam would, invariably on the late turn of 1p.m. to 10p.m., use our teak break, which was 5p.m. until 6p.m., to go to Tyseley Station in order to watch the 4p.m. London train negotiate the points and crossings at the south end of the station. The tremendous roll and lurch of the locomotive at this point fascinated us in no small degree, and frequently elicited gasps of awe and wonder. As this was usually at two minutes to six, it meant a very speedy dash back to the locomotive office to get our checks out by 6p.m. We were very often the subject of a reprimand for reporting a minute late, and frequently were both to experience that same performance as firemen and, later, drivers.

To return to our specific job of engine cleaning, all those fine locomotives were turned out like brand-new cars. Attention was paid to the copper chimney top, brass safety-valve cover, nameplates, beading, steelwork and the beautiful Brunswick Green livery and ornate lining and, of course, the very fine insignia of the Great Western Railway and the combined arms of the cities of London and Bristol.

If we knew of a particular driver who would be coming to take the engine we were cleaning off the shed, we scarpered before he came, as on arrival, he would possibly give an appraising look at his mount and then look for any points we had inadvertently missed. He had been known to feel the backs of the spokes of the large coupled wheels for any traces of dirt or oil; such was the standard expected and maintained. In this connection, I remember being 'hauled over the coals' regarding a complaint by the driver of an engine which had just left the shed and was taking water outside. The complaint was that the back tender coupling had not been properly polished, and I was instructed to proceed immediately to remedy the omission. As I was polishing the offending article, I said to Jack, who was by my side, 'anyone would think she was going on exhibition in a jeweller's shop', and I was unaware that the driver, one of the old brigade, was standing right behind me and overhead my remarks. His observations concerning them were, to say the least, very caustic. The cleaner, in the main, despite the laborious and frequently dirty jobs, would stand back and admire his handiwork; the finished locomotive in all her pristine glory. Many times the cleaners wished that the time would come when they could go with the locomotive on her journey.

My five years of engine cleaning eventually passed, and the great day arrived when I was instructed to proceed to the 'Holy of Holies', Park House in Swindon, the portals of which I was to enter many times during my career on the footplate. Many footplate aspirants have entered and left very dejected on being turned down, unable to pass the most rigorous examination required for footplate work, and I was to be reminded of this, very forcibly, on several occasions during my career.

The high standard required was, of course, justified in view of the demands made on one's physical powers with respect to the nature of the work. In any weather, with always irregular hours, frequent night duty and the rough and tumble of locomotive working, it was certainly no job for a weakling. There was, as I have said, a slogan in those days 'only the best is good enough for the Great Western' and in no place was it more vehemently expressed than at Park House. The stringent eyesight test comprised letter cards, coloured lights and coloured wools, which I passed 6 – 6 in both eyes. On the GWR this eyesight test was repeated every five years, or more frequently, in the case of a man off sick or involved in an accident; this maintained a very high standard of fitness for men on the main line.

On 6th June 1924 my foot was on the bottom rung of the Great Western ladder. I was issued with overalls, uniform cap (commonly known as a 'main liner'), small coat and overcoat, resplendent with the GWR monogram in red; I felt two feet taller. In addition I was also given a number, 21253, which I was to retain throughout my railway career.

Many and varied were the stories from successful candidates returning from Park House, of their ordeal with the Company doctor, and the extremely meticulous eyesight tests, and it was with some trepidation that I proceeded to Swindon. However, everything turned out fine, and I returned in a state of great elation and prepared to commence the career of my boyhood dreams which, alas, as events proved, I was never to realise in its entirety; but for the moment I was walking on air.

The examiner, on advising me that I had passed as a registered fireman, gave me a small book with the injunction to read, mark, learn and inwardly digest all it contained; this being the Rules and Regulations of the Great Western Railway. Despite the injunction, however, there are still a few passages I have yet to assimilate, and this small book is by my side as I write!

On the cover and flyleaf of this book I listed the names of all the men I was to be associated with in my capacity as fireman for the next eighteen years although, of course, at the time, I was not aware I should be spending such a lengthy period with the shovel. Delayed promotion was largely due to the tremendous industrial depression of the 1920s and 1930s which affected the Company's business and, in turn, affected the chance of early promotion.

Returning to my list, it contains the names of men of varying character and philosophy. Each and all had their own ideas of how a locomotive should be worked, and no two men worked exactly alike. However, they all had one feature in common, an abiding dedication to their job. They were, to me, a race apart, and regarded their mounts in the same way as the old-time cavalry soldier regarded his horse, with the greatest affection and esteem. They expected the same attention to duty from their firemen, particularly in the case of boiler control. If a boiler was pressed at 250p.s.i., they expected the fireman to keep 249¾p.s.i., a feat only possible after long experience and knowledge of the road. It could be most disconcerting to a driver, when running into a station or up to an adverse signal, to have his vision obscured by steam escaping from the safety-valves and, of course, running into a terminal station, it was most important to keep the boiler quiet in view of the public address system. It was a case of, as regards the fireman, correct anticipation of the demands made on the boiler. A good head of steam was required when the locomotive was working and quiescence when the locomotive was standing, and in this connection I remember the practice, in the London Division, of using train engines to pull long, heavy and empty trains into Paddington Station, before commencing their own particular job. I have spent several anxious moments under these circumstances, as we were often booked away almost as soon as the train in front had departed, and keeping a boiler under control, with a huge fire ready to cope with our own heavy train, required some judicious handling, as any noise or smoke in Paddington Station was absolutely taboo, and any deviation was quickly brought to the attention of the Locomotive Inspector.

All these good men on my list, to the best of my knowledge, have now passed on, possibly to join that great Valhalla of enginemen, if there is such a place.

My last mate, Ralph, of Wrexham, passed away aged over ninety only a short time ago. We shared some very interesting experiences together during my last few months as a fireman on the Cardiff run on both routes, from Birmingham via Stratford-upon-Avon in the one case, and via Worcester and Hereford in the other. The GWR at that time ran a very extensive service, both in direction and routes, despite the fact that this was wartime, with everything in short supply including, at that time, the precious commodities of tea and sugar. Because of this, we cultivated an acquaintance with an old lady who had temporariy taken charge of the refreshment rooms at Worcester (Foregate Street), and in exchange for a large bucket of coal, our billycan was filled with tea, which sustained us during the long heavy drag up through the Malverns and to Hereford.

The 3.48p.m. service from Birmingham was a trip I well remember, as we almost ran into real trouble approaching Ledbury Tunnel box. There was always a compulsory dead stop at this point, due to the special regulations governing the passage of trains through the single line of Ledbury Tunnel, and a very interesting arrangement, specially authorised at that time by the Ministry of Transport, enabled trains to be worked through the tunnel on a single line without a staff. In order to obviate any irregularity or possible accident, the signalling arrangements between the boxes at each end of the tunnel were very stringent indeed. All trains were required to stop dead before being allowed on to the single line after 'line clear' had, of course, been received. As a further precaution against accident, the points controlling the entry on to the single line were set towards a short length of line terminating in a sand drag on a very sharply rising gradient. With this in mind, we were approaching the distant signal which was at 'caution', and Ralph attempted to close the regulator and bring the train under control prior to the compulsory stop. Several attempts on his part failed to close the regulator, whilst the distance to the stop was rapidly diminishing. Finally, after partially succeeding in closing the regulator, he put the reversing screw handle into mid-gear and was able to stop the engine, and we both spent a few anxious moments before we brought the locomotive under control. The engine was subseqently examined at Tyseley, and the stripping down revealed a slightly bent regulator rod; the locomotive was No. 4939.

Ledbury Tunnel, situated at the summit of a long rising gradient, could be quite an ordeal to work through, especially with a long heavy train. It was a very old structure, totally unsuitable for working with modern engines, as the clearance above the chimney top was a matter of a few inches, and the conditions when passing through with the locomotive working at maximum effort could be very trying indeed, with the exhaust beating down making breathing very difficult. It was always a practice with Ralph and I to raise the fall plate, that is the connecting plate between engine and tender, in order to induce a draught of air to disperse the choking smoke and steam, although, invariably, we had recourse to a handkerchief over the mouth and nose. No firing was possible in the tunnel, of course, and the fire had to be made up to keep the boiler well up to meet the demands of the very heavy working of the engine. Under these conditions the rail could also be very greasy, and we always had to be on the alert to prevent and anticipate slipping. An engine slipping under these cirumstances, on a sharply rising gradient, could be very serious indeed, as persistent slipping could bring the train to a stand, and should this happen, it would be extremely difficult to get away.

Banking engines were employed where required, and it can be appreciated that the men who were assisting in the rear frequently had a rough time with their own smoke and exhaust, in addition to that of the train engine. To somewhat alleviate the arduous nature of bank engine working, an arrangement was fitted for both men to facilitate breathing. This took the form of a dish and pipe leading down towards the ballast and, if conditions got too bad, both driver and fireman had to rely on air through this method. However, leading or banking, we were always relieved to come out into clean fresh air, and an indication of the conditions we worked through were shown on all the brasswork in the cab, and elsewhere.

The alternative route via Stratford-upon-Avon to Cardiff was a push-over by comparison, and, as a general rule, a good ride. The train left Snow Hill at 9.20a.m. with the first stop being at Stratford, where there was a quick intake of water, then Cheltenham, Gloucester, Newport and Cardiff. This allowed a quick turn round on the shed, and a chance to eat a well-earned lunch before the trip back in the early afternoon.

On the return journey we had the same stops, but had to top

up the tender tank at Magar troughs before the romp through Newport and Gloucester to home. However, this trip presented a very different aspect as regards gradients, the 'down' trip, by comparison, being a free wheel. It is almost level to Gloucester requiring the minimum of effort from the locomotive to keep time, but after Gloucester there was a continuous rise to Cheltenham (Lansdown). After this the gradient continues to rise with the Cotswolds on our right, always a lovely sight at any time of the year. We then go through Winchcombe and over the top at Toddington, then away on the slight fall to Broadway and Stratford-upon-Avon, our last stop before Birmingham. Immediately on leaving Stratford, we faced a sharp incline, well within the capabilities of our mount, and up to Wilmecote on the level, streaking through Bearley and a good run up to Henley-in-Arden, at the foot of a long sharp climb to Earlswood Lakes at the summit. After this we had an easy run to Hall Green, and the speed had to be brought down for the junction at Tyseley South, and then the final run into Birmingham (Snow Hill). These trips were always a pleasure to work, with the locomotive in the very capable hands of Ralph. So, after eighteen years with a shovel, my firing days came to an end in 1942.

When I left Ralph, he gave me an old silver watch as a token of his appreciation of our times together, but shortly after my appointment to engineman, I responded to an appeal by the management to under-take supervisory duties, and was accepted; because of this Ralph 'cut me dead'. He had, I know, a distinct aversion to what he called the 'hard hat brigade', but I am happy to say that when I eventually assumed my normal duties, diplomatic relations were resumed and these remained right through to retirement.

I mentioned previously that Ralph had passed away quite recently at the very ripe old age of ninety plus, and so another of the dwindling number of men, who, as cleaners, we facetiously referred to as one of the 'old brigade' passed on. In the earlier years of the century these selfsame men had laid the foundations of better pay and conditions, including a shorter working week of 48 instead of 72 hours. They also fought a long uphill battle to obtain greater parti-cipation in consultations with management, which culminated in a complete new appraisal of relations between management and men. Through the medium of this new negotiating machinery, many anomalies were resolved to the benefit of the workmen.

I am of the opinion that it would not be out of place here to mention that implement which loomed so largely in my duties as fireman, the shovel. I was extremely careful to ensure that I had at least one good tool before leaving the shed, and always a second shovel in reserve, bearing in mind my previous experience when, as a very young and inexperienced fireman, I deposited both coal and shovel in the firebox! My embarrassment, and also the remarks made by the driver, can be imagined. For ever afterwards, it was two shovels for me, just in case!

The ideal shovel was about 20in. long by about 9in. wide, and to improve the use of same, the ends were cut slightly back to make it easier for the transferring of coal into the firebox and, with practice, the shovel could be turned over with a deft 'flick of the wrist' when firing. It had other uses, too, apart from that of moving coal. It made an excellent frying pan, and I still remember the innumerable occasions, when time allowed, of the beautiful aroma of bacon and eggs which arose in the course of cooking. It also made a very efficient wash-basin, always being brought into service at the end of a trip. Packed up with a piece of coal at the end, it would hold just enough water for a decent wash. Hot water was provided from the coal watering pipe attached to the boiler feed, known to locomotivemen as the 'pet pipe'. Using the shovel as a frying pan and wash-basin had been the practice since time immemorial, until some misguided individual, with possibly an eye on promotion, suggested to the management that two holes be drilled in every shovel. This idea was adopted, and bang went the possibilities of the 'shovel cum frying pan cum wash-basin'.

My association with Ralph, at that particular time was years away, and I was to be associated with many men on my progress through the links. Each link was a group of jobs catering for every type of work at the depot, and the newly-appointed fireman started on what we called the 'pilot or shunting link'. We graduated as vacancies occurred in each link, with the senior fireman in each group or link moving up.

CHAPTER TWO

Chris and Fred

The first two years were spent at Bordesley Junction, a very large yard with six shunting engines working continuously round the clock, seven days a week, and it was here, under the watchful eye of Chris, that I began my firing career. There was nothing spectacular in shunting duties, but I was on the first rung with a good and interesting mate.

It was around this time that I contemplated getting married. Under the terms of my appointment as fireman, I was obliged to move away from home and reside in the calling up area within two miles of the shed. So I reasoned that if I had to move, we may as well set up home, which would be far better than lodgings. On 6th September 1924 we were married and, believe it or not, I had to apply for the day off to do so. I had previously applied for the time off, but apparently the application had 'gone astray', and it was not until we made the customary enquiry in respect of our next turn of duty that I was advised that I was on the same turn. 'But I'm getting married tomorrow, Saturday', brought no favourable response, and it was only after seeing the foreman on duty that I was granted the day off.

We went on a weekend honeymoon and I was back on duty at 10p.m. Monday. In 1926 I was moved to the main depot of Tyseley, and made my acquaintance with an outstanding character by the name of Fred, with whom I stayed for some five years. During this period, I was to have many experiences, including my first 'double home' trip, of which I will say more later.

I was indebted to Fred for his patience in demonstrating the finer points of firing coal, the correct manipulation of the shovel, the ability to direct coal to any given point in the firebox and the correct method of handling a boiler to meet the varying conditions of load and road. To him, and later to me, firing was almost an exact science, which stood me in good stead when I progressed through the links to higher grade work, and was associated with men who demanded a meticulous standard, and who would brook no deviations from their own particular method of working. There were also many enginemen who insisted upon a certain type of fire. It was usual with the very large fireboxes to build and maintain a big fire, that is, a very large 'tump' beginning at the fire hole door, and sloping right down to the front of the box, and the basis of firing was continual feeding of the back, with the result that fuel was fed to sides and front.

Particular attention had also to be paid to the front of the firebox, to prevent the fire getting too thin and drawing air, thus causing poor combustion of the mass of fire, and resulting in poor steaming. No doubt my contemporaries will recall the axiom with regard to this 'always look after the front, the back will reflect immediately the state of the front'.

Locomotives of the 43XX type, of which we had several, which required special nursing, had a particular type of firebox, and tended to be fired too heavily towards the front, and in consequence the fire became blacked with poor steaming resulting. Recourse had to be made to the use of the pricker bar, a practice frowned upon by most enginemen, as it tended to force the clinker into the bars, and further mar the poor steaming qualities of the fire. The usual comment from the driver was 'you get steam from the shovel, mate, not the poker'.

Many enginemen, even in the case of the large fireboxes, insisted on the fireman working a side fire, in effect, firing both sides of the box and keeping the back corners full up. Certainly, this method presented a greater surface of live fire and definitely gave good results, but it was indeed much harder work for the fireman on a long and heavy trip.

In the main the best South Wales coal was used on all express work, both goods and passenger. The quality of this coal has no equal throughout the world for steam raising, but it had to be fired right, with no two shovelsful in the same place at one time. 'Mr Engineman Meticulous' could always tell by the colour of the exhaust whether the coal had been applied correctly, or whether it had been shovelled on 'upside down'.

With Fred's guidance, I gradually learned the finer points of the game, and had ample opportunity to demonstrate my appreciation due to the fact that he signed the road to routes outside our usual roster, something allowed by the management at that time, and the fact that Fred had signed the road to Banbury and Gloucester, gave me my aforesaid chance. However, the first time I worked 'double home' to Gloucester clearly showed I still had a long way to go. Fred had the bumps following this abject failure of mine, which made me more determined than ever to prevent a similar occurrence.

This particular job involved the working of a train of empty 'mex' or cattle wagons for Fishguard, and the engine booked to us was No. 2392, a standard goods 0-6-0. It was with high spirits that I booked on for the job, this being my maiden trip 'double home'.

After a careful examination of the locomotive, the smokebox and such like, and on looking underneath at the ash pan, I noticed the fire did not show too clearly through the bars. On imparting this information to Fred, he said that the shed foreman had told him that the engine had been out for a short trip previously, and did not warrant its fire being cleaned. His advice to me was to 'See that you have a good chisel bar on her and you will be okay', so off we went.

Everything went all right to Stratford-upon-Avon where we stopped for water, and I took the opportunity to give the fire a good 'root up' with the chisel bar to open up the clinker, which had started to assume quite solid proportions, and was considerably more than I would have assumed should have accumulated from our start. It became increasingly obvious to me that the fire was far dirtier than we first thought. However, we left Stratford with a 'pot full', and I managed to hold my own to Toddington where we stopped for examination of the train.

By this time, the fire was looking anything but rosy. However, away we went after a good blow up, but I was steadily losing ground, with the water now half-way up the glass and a very poor head of steam. It was here that Fred decided to have a go with very indifferent results and finally, at Gotherington, at the top the bank and with the water almost out of sight, we had to stop. If Fred had taken the train on any further, we should have dropped a plug, that is the fusible plug in the roof of the firebox. I was almost frantic with shame and disappointment at the thought of letting my mate down, but I still think (and plead in extenuation) that if we had started with a really clean fire, things would have been different.

So there we were, stuck in the section. The guard came up as per regulations and asked what the trouble was. Fred assured him that in ten minutes we would be away, when we had sufficient water in the boiler to go down the bank. The guard went back to his van, greatly relieved that he would not be required to protect the train in the rear because if we had been stopped much longer, he would have been required to do so.

After much poking, and the use of the blower with a very judicious few shovelfuls of coal, sufficient water was injected into the boiler to enable us to proceed. It was fortunate that due to the profile of the line, very little steam was required to work the train, it being almost a free wheel to Cheltenham and Gloucester, by which time I had got her round with a full pot; I was extremely pleased when the relief crew stepped on the footplate.

After Fred advised the driver of our difficulties, they proceeded on their journey. We learned afterwards, through a very stinging report, that they only got as far as Bullo Pill when the engine was taken on the shed for the fire to be cleaned. We booked off at Gloucester Shed and thus ended my first 'double home' trip, on which I had set out with such excitement and high hopes. Fred was extremely magnanimous, just the man he was, and commiserated with me on an unfortunate occurrence, taking the blame for the initial bad start on the shed. In self defence, I can only reiterate that I did mention the condition of the fire at the time.

It was with Fred that I came up against established officialdom, in the form of an enquiry in respect of an incident in connection with working a passenger train. I had been on quite a few minor enquiries in my cleaning days when very meticulous chargeman cleaners had reported us for one misdemeanour or another, arising from the exuberance that invaribly occurs with a crowd such as we were. Card games in our meal times were absolutely taboo and it was a walk 'down the passage' for anyone caught in the act. There were also cases where we were hauled before the 'beak' when discovered sleeping in the firebox in a warm cripple, amongst many other cases too numerous to mention. Usually, it was a verbal caution as to our future conduct, very soon to be forgotten.

The incident with Fred was quite another matter, and it was with considerable apprehension that I was advised of the enquiry into the irregularity. The circumstances were as follows: at that time in 1926 we could be booked for four hours on a Sunday to complete the set working of say a passenger roster, work the short trip to Leamington or Stratford and back, and book off on arrival at the shed. This meant a spoiled weekend without the benefit of a full working day at the enhanced rate for Sunday duty.

On this particular occasion and, incidentally, my first passenger job, we booked on at about 6p.m. to relieve a regular passenger driver who had his own engine, a 51XX 2-6-2. He did not relish the idea of giving his engine up to two bottom link men, but he had no option. Everything on the footplate was beautiful and in good order so away we went, after getting the 'right away' from our guard, the next stop being Spring Road. When we stopped there I started to apply the handbrake to hold the train steady and was promptly told to leave it which, of course, as there is only one Captain of a ship, I obeyed. At the same time, I was aware that it was against regulations.

At Hall Green, our next stop, Fred ran smartly into the platform and when the train came to a stand, proceeded to recreate the vacuum ready for a quick getaway. These local trains were very sharply timed, and to keep time it was necessary to be ready as soon as the guard gave the green light. However, before the signal was given, the engine started to move away and Fred had to apply the brake. The guard who was on his side immediately exhibited a red light, and continued to do so whilst he walked the length of the train up to the engine.

It appeared that when the train inadvertently started, a lady passenger was in the act of alighting and her husband was standing on the platform helping her down. To make matters a thousand times worse, the lady was far advanced in a certain condition and, naturally, her husband took a very dim view of the proceedings and before we were allowed to continue our journey, names were taken for future reference. Fred, of course, had to make out a report on the shed, and attributed the occurrence to a regulator not closing properly. In point of fact the regulator was so well lubricated that if it were slammed shut, it was quite possible to spring open a little way sufficient to move a train on the level.

The report the guard was obliged to make, and the possible consequences of injury to the passenger and the company's liability, necessitated the examination of the engine for any possible regulator fault. The feelings of the driver whose engine it was can well be imagined, and it was an extremely angry man who confronted Fred next day and told him that his engine was to be stripped down to locate any regulator fault. As a matter of fact the Depot Master himself, when viewing the regulator valve on the bench, moved it in its slide with an ordinary pencil, thus obviating any possibility of the regulator not closing properly in service. So we were for it, and were advised of the enquiry at an early date.

Presiding at the enquiry was the Assistant Divisional Superintendent, Mr Webb, together with his clerk and the Depot Master. The guard was called first and gave his version, after which Fred was called and, in the procedure which followed, he cleared me by accepting the blame for the whole affair and, in view of the material evidence in the perfect condition of the regulator, he could not take any other course. Also, in view of the fact that there were to be no claims made by the passenger, Fred received what amounted to a verbal caution and advised as to his future conduct. I was then called and moved into the 'presence' with the greatest trepidation, visualising all kinds of dire penalties. Mr Webb looked at me hard and long and then said 'in this irregularity at Hall Green you let your mate down, don't let it happen again'. Not being aware of what had passed between him and Fred, I just held my tongue and let him more or less burn me up. I could have informed him that I had been instructed to leave the handbrake alone, but such a cause would have been unthinkable, and I got away with some very caustic remarks concerning my future conduct.

25

A very interesting sequel took place fifteen years after this interview when, in my capacity of mens' representative, I met him in round table meetings to discuss matters arising and affecting the general working of the shed. Mr Webb was now the Divisional Superintendent, and our relations were, in the main, extremely cordial. On more than one occasion, he would hand my colleague and I his cigarette case, which we almost emptied during the sometimes very protracted discusions. On these occasions, I was reminded of the somewhat accrimonious interview of years ago. Such is life!

Fred was the instigtor of the billycan, whereby a very nice cup of 'char' could be made under almost all conditions. From time immemorial it had been the practise for footplate crews to carry a bottle, usually a Johnny Walker whisky bottle, filled with cold tea but with no milk or sugar, a concoction having not the remotest relation to the 'cuppa'. The majority of the older men carried a stone jar containing this very dubious mixture, and apparently this practise went back to the dark ages. I recall when, at times, I was spare and went with one of the old brigade on a job, that my mate would look askance at my teamaking, when the occasion arose, and although he could not reasonably forbid it, he muttered in his beard that he didn't know what the world was coming to.

Fred's teamaking occasioned many facetious remarks from the rest of the footplate fraternity but gradually, and with the exception of the older men, it became part and parcel of the engine crews' equipment. I believe the practice really started with the London Old Oak men or possibly Reading crews, and I have observed on many occasions the very generous proportions of their billycans, holding up to three and sometimes four pints. A good brew up could be made under all sorts of conditions, and I have even made a cuppa on a fast train but, of course, this performance could only be carried out with the co-operation of the driver, and under suitable conditions.

The back of the fire, extending level with the fire hole ring, would be flattened down to make a bed for the billycan, which would have previously had a generous coating of oil on the outside to prevent burning, and a matchstick was placed on top of the water to prevent the water being smoked. At a suitable stretch of road, Fred would ease the regulator right down, and with one eye on the road ahead, prepare to shoot the 'mashing' into the boiling water as I withdrew the can from the fire with the aid of a tommy bar. Then, with mash extracted and can wiped clean we were away full belt to the business in hand, with a very nice cuppa to sustain us. A thousand times better than the old square bottle and its poor contents.

In this connection it is worthwhile recording an incident that occurred just after I left Fred, from whom I received a presumably true account of the proceedings. His new mate, by reputation, could be very facetious in his general conversation, which sometimes got him into trouble and certainly, in this particular incident, the effect was extremely disappointing to himself and Fred.

The turn was the 3.05a.m. Bordesley Junction to Stourbridge, which meant the engine was booked off the shed at 2.45p.m., twenty minutes before train departure time. The general idea was to get to the departure point in good time, to make the much needed cuppa after a busy hour on the shed preparing the engine. On this occasion the morning was bitterly cold with a very sharp frost, rendering a nice cup of hot steaming tea even more desirable, especially Fred's brew. Fred duly backed on to the train and Jack, his fireman, made the tea, wiped the can, extracted the match and applied the milk. The whole inviting concoction was now ready for consumption and was placed on what we call the dish; the small shelf just beneath the regulator. Jack was in the tender breaking up the large lumps of coal, whilst Fred was making a start on his daily record by the light of a flare lamp. The guard then arrived to advise Fred of the load, and the following dialogue took place:

Gary (the guard) 'Good morning Fred, a full cargo, 35 number ones, Stourbridge'.
Fred 'Morning Gary, okay, cold enough for a walking stick, like a nice cup of tea?'
Gary 'By gum, just what the doctor ordered on a morning like this.'

He then mounted the footplate, where he helped himself to a nice cup of tea. The cup, by the way, was one of a large set bearing the GWR monogram. Fred was still writing and Jack was still cracking lumps when Gary said 'what shall I do with the tea?' as he had been holding the billycan in the one hand while he held the cup in the other, and did not know exactly where to deposit the can. Jack replied nonchalantly 'Oh throw the rest over the side' and Gary, without thinking, threw the contents over the side to the utter consternation of Fred and his mate, who were just about to enjoy a nice cup of tea before starting on the trip. This goes to show that an over abundance of facetiousness carried its penalties.

Gary, with the most profound apologies, beat a hasty retreat to his van while Fred addressed himself very strongly to Jack on the advisability of controlling his 'glib' tongue, lest people take him too literally.

I was to remain with Fred for the next four years, chiefly on local work with the occasional trip to Banbury or Gloucester 'double home'. Fred, apart from his prowess as a fireman, was an extremely good entertainer, always with an abundance of stories, some of which would not be admissible in a drawing room. It can be imagined that when we were in the cabin waiting for relief work he was always the centre of attraction, and he also had a great fund of tales regarding his adventures in the Middle East where he served during World War I with the Railway Operating Division. Due to these travels in Egypt, he acquired the pseudonym of Abdull, a verbal appendage he retained throughout his life.

Just about this time, a cleaner came on transfer to Tyseley from Aberbeeg. Due to the passage of time I forget his name, but as a Welshman he had the national fervour and enthusiasm for singing. It was not long before he started a Male Voice Choir, not really difficult in view of the very large number of Welshmen employed at our depot, and for many years it flourished. Many retirement concerts saw us doing our stuff, as Fred and I also joined. We were both extremely fond of singing but Fred on these occasions surpassed himself as the comic relief, and many convivial evenings were enjoyed when Tom, Dick or Harry retired.

On one particular night, when two of our most respected members were retiring, we had among other items a great favourite of ours, 'Comrades in Arms' which always went down well with our audience. However, on this particular occasion due, possibly, to an over indulgence of the bottle or glass, we rendered 'Comrades in Arms' with unusual gusto, so much so that we ran away with the conductor who, for appearances sake, had to beat time to our singing instead of the choir following the lead of his baton. Despite this, the performance went down very well, with the listeners unaware that, for once, the singers were leading the conductor. After the performance he took us on one side and told us in no uncertain terms just what he thought of us.

CHAPTER THREE

Alf

I left Fred in 1930 and worked a few months with Sid, an extremely meticulous engineman who liked things just so, but a very good mate to work with all the same. This link was what we called the third class link, involving more local goods trains and passenger work. After Sid I went with Alf, and was to remain with him for the next four years. Alf, in common with the majority of enginemen, liked things done according to the book. He was a first class driver and hated the tiniest bit of dust, but during the whole of the four years, we got on famously. The work now was extremely varied, with the link involving 38 different jobs mostly local goods and pick-up work, within an area including Leamington, Stratford, Stourbridge and Wolverhampton. If we had a sticky job at times, there was always the consolation that it only occurred once in 38 weeks.

It was about this time in 1930 that an incident occurred involving an express passenger train which, due to the most unusual nature of the accident, has remained in my memory to this day, and merits more than a passing mention.

The express, known to us as the 'Down Dover' and due in Birmingham (Snow Hill) at 3.10p.m., was passing Alton Reservoir at 70 m.p.h. when the leading coupled wheel became detached and was thrown on to the reservoir bank. The remarkable fact was, that this huge wheel of 6ft. 8½in. was normally working behind a mass of mechanism, including the very heavy connecting rod and also the slide bars and piston crosshead. This great wheel, one of six on the locomotive was, by some miracle, thrown clear. Had the wheel gone under the locomotive it would immediately have turned the engine over and a major accident could not have been avoided, the train being full of passengers. I had ample opportunity next day, Sunday, to examine the locomotive and to this day, I still maintain it was one of the most remarkable cases on record of a locomotive losing a wheel of this size and remaining on the rails. The driver, with commendable promptitude, brought the train to a stop and great was his astonishment when he saw the damage and a wheel missing.

I am indebted to the Birmingham Reference Library for their kindness in providing me with a photostat copy of the account in the Birmingham newspapers, the copy also showing the locomotive with the wheel missing. I recall also that this same paper carried a photograph of the wheel lying on the bank of Alton Reservoir but, due to unknown circumstances, this is not available.

Much of my work with Alf involved night duty, of which during the whole of my career, I was never fond. However, this type of work was necessary in view of the demands made on the existing system during the daytime hours, the Midlands being one of the most densely worked areas of the country due to the intensive working of local passenger and express services. Hence the incidence of night duty for us in the third class link.

The major part of our particular jobs took us through Snow Hill Tunnel, and this presented some unusual features. The tunnel itself runs underneath the city centre and the ruling gradient is extremely severe, rising towards the station end at 1 in 60 or less. In order to obviate any possibility of a train being unable to negotiate this extremely sharp bank, special operating conditions were in force. In point of fact the tunnel was approached by a falling gradient of about a mile and this allowed the driver to obtain sufficient momentum with the train to carry it up through the tunnel, and as the majority of goods and mineral trains started from Bordesley Junction South box, special arrangements were in operation to allow this to be done.

No fully laden train was allowed to leave the South signal box unless 'line clear' had been obtained throughout the entire section including Bordesley South, Bordesley North, Moor Street and Birmingham North, the last named box being at the Birmingham end of the tunnel, and the top of the incline on entering Snow Hill Station.

The load for a C class 57XX locomotive was 27 No. 1s, that is wagons containing 12 tons of coal, while for a D class 31XX or 43XX, 35 No. 1s were the norm. In view of these exceptional circumstances, the conditions respecting the fire had to be just right, as it would have been a waste of time attempting the run with a dirty or an inadequately prepared fire. Of course, should a train fail to get up through the tunnel a delay would occur involving following traffic, as the timetable involved average working through the tunnel of a train every five minutes. Indeed, there were lengthy periods when a goods train didn't stand a chance during the rush hours.

It behoved every crew, when taking an engine off the shed, to see that everything had been done to ensure a good trip through this particular section, particularly with regard to the fireman who had to build a fire that would stand up to the terrific punching demanded to keep the boiler pressure at the maximum. A really good fairly thick fire, built up on the shed, had burned through by the time we had run the two miles to our starting point. So when we had the road, a good 'root' up with the pricker meant the engine was bounding flat out, lever well back, regulator invariably wide open, and 'hell for leather' towards the tunnel. By the time we were well into the incline the lever was in the corner, and we were breasting the tape with great staccato exhaust into Snow Hill passenger station.

A further load was placed on the locomotive due to the fact that the guard, at one specific point during our rush, had to apply his handbrake hard on to keep the couplings tight on the back end of the train, the front end now ascending the tunnel incline and the back end of the train on a falling gradient, thus preventing a breakaway. He, of course, released his brake when the whole train was on the incline. Catch points connected to a sand drag were positioned at the Moor Street end of the tunnel to divert any such breakaway. This was a Ministry of Transport requirement to obviate any conflicting movement of trains out of Moor Street, a very busy station serving suburban trains. It can be rightly assumed then that this particular section of line required the utmost co-operation of the engine crew for a successful trip through the 'hole', and a very serious report would follow if any driver failed to negotiate the tunnel.

With Alf, I worked my way through the link, working trains locally to the north, south, east and west. Some of these local goods trains required specific treatment on what we called the Black Country jobs, and with a fairly long train it was possible, due to the contour of the road, to have the train on three different gradients at once, which called for a very careful use of the handbrake to prevent a breakaway. The so-called Black Country was, at that time, a very lucrative source of revenue with its collieries and steelworks, and at any time during the 24 hours of any day, it was always a hive of activity.

A turn of duty in this particular link is worth recalling. This was a turn I really hated, as it involved booking on at 1.50a.m., 2.50a.m. off the shed, for what we called the 'Kiddy', really the 3.05a.m. Stourbridge service, with our mount invariably a 51XX or 43XX, both D classification. We would be taking a full load through the tunnel and Handsworth Bank, with a compulsory stop at Rowley Regis for brakes on the train. Due to the gradient of 1 in 60 it was very necessary to have the assistance of brakes on the train to prevent it getting out of control. The train was steamed on to the summit of the incline while the guard applied brakes on the wagons and when the driver was satisfied that sufficient brakes were on, he would give two short sharp whistles and the guard would regain the train in his van. The train then proceeded down this long and steep bank with the engine and guard's brake held in reserve, and at the foot of the bank the train was brought to a stand and the brakes released. Modern day practice has eliminated this method of descending banks, as almost all goods and mineral wagons have the airbrake worked from the locomotive. Thus the driver has the whole of the train at his disposal for braking purposes, and the standard rules for incline working have been largely superseded.

The 7.05 ex-Stourbridge passenger service was the return working of this turn of duty. This was one of the heaviest trains hauled over that section of line, and with a load of usually nine coaches, with a tare of something like 280 tons, it required an all-out effort from the locomotive and the engine crew. This train was booked to call at Old Hill, positioned on the steepest part of the bank which, as I explained, was 1 in 60 and as railways go, is a very steep gradient indeed. It is worth recording that the locomotive sometimes started away on what we enginemen called 'on one side' that is, due to the setting of the cranks and valve gear, the engine could come to a stand with one side momentarily closed to steam. It amply demonstrated the colossal power pent up in the boiler, enabling the heavy train to be started under these conditions. I may add, however, that the pressure had to be well on the mark, otherwise it was a waste of time to try to get away, and it was a combined effort to get away with this exceptionally heavy train. With the train brakes blown off and the fireman holding the train on the handbrake, as soon as the 'right away' was given the regulator was opened wide whilst the fireman released the handbrake. We used to call this particular job carrying anything up to a thousand passengers, the coal train.

CHAPTER FOUR

George

Alf and I got along very well and the years passed all too quickly until about 1936 when I was promoted to the next link, the London link. Here I met George who was a unique character, a superb engineman and a 'rough diamond' with a quaint expression of speech, often strongly used to meet a variety of circumstances. He was also a Brummie, and I do not write in any way disparagingly of that ilk, but in this connection, George was wont to express himself in regard to the majority of engine crews at Tyseley who were, to him, foreigners, that is, men from all over the Western system. In point of fact only half a dozen of us amongst several hundred drivers and firemen were natives of Birmingham, I myself being a native of that city.

In those days all men promoted to driver or fireman were moved from their home station, and it was very rare for man to be retained at his home station. Consequently Tyseley was, in the main, as with most GWR depots, worked by men away from their native place. George's first remarks to me on our initial turn of duty was 'this is where you start earning your living sonny boy' and I often wondered afterwards what he thought I had been doing for the last ten years or so. He was, of course, referring to the work on 'them there Black Country jobs', the nature of which was not comparable to my new duties in the London link.

It was with George that I made my maiden trip to London, a half-day excursion to Paddington, leaving Birmingham at 10a.m. and arriving at Paddington at 12.13p.m. We were due away from Paddington at 8.10p.m., to run into Birmingham at 10.15p.m. The return fare for eight hours in the Metropolis was 6s. 0d. and the train, a regular Sunday runner, was crowded. It was a beautiful hot summer day and a marvellous trip and, for the benefit of any one time 'number snatchers', the locomotive was No. 5955 *Garth Hall*, a good runner and an equally good steamer.

When George brought the great locomotive to a stand just inside the 'lawn' at Paddington, his first act was to take a small circular mirror from his waistcoat pocket, and in the best 'Brummie' English he said "Ow 'av you got me 'ere, you toffee-nosed so and so?'. He had hardly a mark on him, whilst I looked like something from the Black and White Minstrel show.

I spent two very interesting years with George and quickly learned to adapt myself to his method of working, and to accept his very unconventional mode of address, either personally or on matters pertaining to the job in hand. Thus 'shape yourself' was invariably used when approaching the water-troughs at speed, no doubt to keep me up to scratch, or 'is she answering the helm'? with regard to the steaming qualities of the boiler, or as a reference to the steam raising qualities of the fireman. In short, his vocabulary was certainly quaint, and his reference to men and matters in general unique. Many times I experienced his philosophy on life and his conduct, when faced with the many vicissitudes, greatly cemented my admiration for him as a first-rate engineman, always capable of meeting any contingency with his usual 'sang froid'.

I may mention here, that picking up water at speed could be a very dicey operation indeed. If the fireman muffed it, a special stop became necessary followed by a report for the driver to answer. Water was picked up by lowering a scoop into a water-filled trough laid between the rails, with the fireman lowering the scoop immediately the engine started to pass over. In the matter of a few seconds, between three and four thousand gallons of water was transferred into the tender tank, and should the fireman leave the scoop down too long, water would cascade from the back of the tender and in the case of a passenger train, the first coach would be drenched, to the distress of any passengers riding in a compartment with the window down.

I well recall one lady passenger who, under these circumstances, claimed for a hat damaged by water. Of course, there was the usual report for the engine crew hence George's admonition when approaching the troughs. However, a few trips enabled me to acquire the trick of good timing, and so it was no longer an ordeal to pass over the troughs at 60m.p.h. and to place and wind the scoop up just at the right moment.

It will be appreciated that water was a very important factor in our work, and the replenishing of the tender on the move and at shed was part and parcel of the job. I may mention in passing, that all London jobs involved taking water by this method no less than three times, at Ruislip, King's Sutton and Rowington.

We took all these jobs in our stride usually making three trips in a week, booking off in London and in for a rest. These were the 'double home' turns, the unfortunate part of a very interesting although at times arduous work, and in this respect I had to work on this type of service for the next five years, a feature not conducive to domestic harmony. However, both George and I spent many interesting hours in London during our enforced period of rest, which, on some jobs, was as long as nineteen hours, and it is fairly true to say that during the two years on these particular jobs, we visited most places of interest in the Metropolis which, of course, illustrates that these rest periods have their advantages. One of the great disadvantages was that it was frequently our experience when arriving back at the lodge to have to wait for an engine crew to get up before we could go to bed. Such an arrangement by today's standards would be unthinkable.

It was around this time that a complete reappraisal of freight services was introduced as a reply to the ever growing competition from the road services, and not a few eyebrows were raised when perusing the new schedules. We men in the London link were particularly affected, as the new jobs and times were largely concerned with the Midlands and London. Among the many changes that I remember, one particular train merits more than a passing reference, and no doubt my contemporaries will remember the 'Park Royal' or the 11.05p.m. Paddington train. This particular train was to consist of seventy fully laden wagons and the time allowed for the 112 miles between Park Royal, London and Hockley, Birmingham, was 180 minutes. To give some idea of the tight timing, the usual London to Birmingham passenger expresses were allowed 120 minutes with a load of 400 tons, usually twelve coaches. The 'Park Royal', with a full 'cargo' of seventy wagons, would have an overall weight of anything up to 1,500 tons, and would be between one eighth and one quarter of a mile in length. This was some job, and I always considered it the roughest three hours work in the Northern Division and although it entailed maximum effort from the engine crew, I always found the experience, of a job well done and invariably to time extremely interesting. The London men had, amongst many trains of this character, one outstanding job called 'The Greenford', commonly called the 'ghost train', which ran from Greenford, Middlesex, to Shrewsbury (145 miles) non-stop.

To return to our 'Park Royal', we had the advantage of a very capable engine in the 47XX 2-8-0 with the No. 4 boiler, similar to that fitted on the 'King' class. The 47XX with a fairly high wheel and a tremendous tractive effort, was quite capable for the job in hand, but she also had a tendency to roll at high speeds rather too much for my liking and, because of this, was considered unsuitable for express passenger work. With the maximum speed of our 'Park Royal' being 50m.p.h., she was well capable of coping without any undue oscillation. Only nine of this particular class were ever built and became known among jokers as the 'owl class', as they only came out at night.

The engine crew working this particular train were required to book on duty at Old Oak Shed at 9.38p.m. for 10.38p.m. off the shed and, needless to say George and I were always there in good time to prepare for the encounter. It was a well-known axiom, and one which I always tried to instil into my firemen, that a good trip is made on the shed and adequate preparation commensurate with the character of the job, were well worthwhile. In any case there was no time after leaving the shed to rectify any omissions that may have been made, so a meticulous examination was made of every salient point before any trip. The driver examining, oiling, feeling and, in general, ensuring that the locomotive was ready for the trip. The fireman, in common with his mate, had many duties to perform with the prospect of a good run which, by any standards, was not the easiest of jobs.

With the smokebox door tightly screwed up and the ashpan clean and free from clinker, tools, fire-irons and two shovels would be checked. The latter would be the most important, as it would not be the first time that I have lost a shovel in the early days through being rather too zealous in my efforts to put a shovelful of coal to the front of the firebox. With the inadvertent loss of a shovel, one could always make a crafty move to get the spare and hope the driver was not looking, that is, of course, if you carried two. Carrying a spare was a practice which I continued throughout my firing career, after the debacle of earlier years in which I lost the 'banjo'.

The fire, of course, merited close attention being, as it were, the 'prime mover' as did the coal in the tender, which was specially coaled for this particular job. After the smokebox door, ashpan, tools, lamps, flags and detonators, the fire claimed attention. As a general rule the fire was at the back of the firebox on arrival and this was poked all over the grate, and it was then built up with fairly large lumps of coal, starting from the front of the box and working back right up to the firehole ring. It was a common enough practice to use anything up to a ton of coal in the process, and all of this great mass of coal would be well burnt through by train time. So by now this great 11ft. 6in. firebox was a great area of fire which, when the locomotive was in motion, would become a huge incandescent mass, which was so vital to meet the demands made on the boiler. Next, while the fire was burning through and the pressure was rising, the fireman devoted the next half hour to breaking up all the large coal in the tender and bringing it forward as much as possible. There was no time to do this on the road once we were away and many times, if we could get under the coal stage, we would ship another ton of small coal to help us on our way.

With the time nearing 10.30p.m. we prepared to leave the shed not forgetting, of course, to take water at the water-column, which would last us to our first pick-up at Ruislip Troughs. George had earlier tested the vacuum brake — an extremely important feature of our impending trip, and we moved up to Old Oak Shed signal where I advised the 'Bobby' by telephone that we were the 11.05 p.m. Paddington train. He then turned us off the shed, tender first, up to Paddington Goods. The fire had burned through by now and pressure was almost on the mark, but we still had another thirty minutes before the commencement of our journey. This was because Paddington allowed only a certain type of traffic and was confined, as a general rule, to half a dozen wagons.

The first two vehicles attached to the engine merit special mention, as they were more or less the forerunners of special container traffic. They were conveyed on this particular train in co-operation with a well-known haulage company — at that time Carter Patison.

At 11.05p.m. prompt we left and cantered down the three miles to Park Royal, where the engine and two containers were detached as we came to a stand. We then crossed over the points and back into Park Royal Yard where we backed on to half our train consisting of 35 wagons, all of which were 'piped' vehicles which were fitted with brakes operable from the locomotive.

With all pipes and couplings connected up George created the vacuum which meant that all air was exhausted from every cylinder, and if no serious leakage was shown on the vacuum gauge in the cab, George indicated that the brake was functioning correctly. The time was 11.30p.m., and we pulled out on to the main line over the points, and back on to the rest of the train. The guard by this time had satisfied himself that all was in order and advised George 'seventy of the best George, and the best of British luck'. So now we had a load of seventy vehicles with an overall weight of between 1,000 and 1,500 tons and a length of between an eighth and a quarter of a mile, and we had around 180 minutes to do the 112 miles non-stop to Hockley in Birmingham. An interesting comparison, the express passenger train was allowed 120 minutes, which meant very little recovery time anywhere and a maximum speed, according to regulations governing this type of train, of 50m.p.h.

With the time coming up to 11.36p.m. and with the starter signal off we were able to proceed, and as we pulled away I exchanged signals with the guard to ensure he was in his van.

The locomotive was getting into her stride at this point, with a little less than full regulator and the lever set at about 45 per cent to get this long heavy train well on the move towards Ruislip. It is there that I should top up the tender tank to take us to King's Sutton, which was our next water pick-up.

The fire was now one huge mass eager for more coal which I applied frequently, keeping the back well up and firing over the top of the huge 'tump' towards the front of the firebox.

The water level was well out of sight in the water gauge frame, and I didn't want to see it come down the glass at any time on the trip. Due to the speed of the locomotive, the water was surging towards the back of the boiler so, even if the level is not visible, it does not indicate that too much water is in the boiler so, as I mentioned, it was advisable to keep the level up and out of sight. Thus a water level half-way down the glass would indicate a serious shortage of water in the boiler, especially during fast running.

To cope with the tremendous demands being made on the boiler water to generate steam, the exhaust injector had to be continuously worked on this class of train, and the fireman's task was by no means lessened by this continual water feed.

The fire is kept well up by using the 'flap', which is an easier method than opening and closing doors. A shovelful of coal flap down, and as soon as the shovel was withdrawn, the flap reverted to an upright position. It can be appreciated the number of times this drill would have to be repeated, when coal consumption worked out at between 70 and 80lb. per mile.

George had now got the train well under way with the regulator set half-way and the lever on 35 per cent. We were now rapidly approaching Ruislip and were by the troughs, so I worked the handle controlling the scoop, remaining ready to work the scoop out of the trough when the tank was almost full. If I misjudged and left the scoop down too long, the result would be a cascade of water all over the footplate, so with 4,000 gallons on the tender, we speeded towards Denham. The distant signal for Gerrards Cross had been given by the bell from the a.t.c. (automatic train control), one of the finest innovations for working these trains, which gave an early indication of the imminent distant signal. This was an extremely important feature, in that a very early indication was given of either 'line clear' or ' warning', this being vital when working trains at high speeds.

It can well be appreciated that particularly in the case of express freight workings, the train must be brought under control immediately an adverse signal is received, and calls for the closest liaison between the driver and fireman. With the regulator closed, the fireman applied his tender brake hard on to bring all wagons up together or buffer to buffer, so that the driver could judiciously apply the vacuum-brake on the whole of the piped vehicles and also, of course, the locomotive's brakes.

This initial move on the part of the fireman was extremely important, because if any sharp application of the brakes was made by the driver there would be the risk of telescoping. Furthermore, the guard would receive a very severe jolt, although it was part of his duty to observe all signals and act accordingly.

There was no peace for the fireman as we passed through Gerrards Cross and Seer Green, with Beaconsfield only minutes away. The pressure was well up when George closed the regulator for the permanent speed restriction of 35m.p.h. through High Wycombe, and allowed the fireman to sit down for a few brief minutes through the restriction.

High Wycombe was reached next, the home of the furniture maker, and we can smell the timber as we approach the station. To digress for a few seconds, it was at this point that I recall a driver in our link who had a report for taking the restriction too fast. Apparently, a passenger in the train's dining car had his soup deposited in his lap, due to violent movement of the coach at excessive speed.

Another good charge of coal all over the firebox as we storm up to Saunderton on a rising gradient, with the locomotive really in its element. With the sharp bark of the exhaust and more coal in the firebox we are really making good time as we pass through Princes Risborough towards Haddenham while rolling and pitching, with the ever present rhythm of wheels over rail joints in the background.

George consulted his Ingersoll watch and shouted across the clamour 'eight minutes down Sonny', but I know from previous experience that given the road we should be there right on time.

Up through Brill, and the locomotive is now being urged a bit more on a rising stretch with more coal, the water level well up out of sight, the exhaust injector still working and boiler pressure almost on the mark at 280p.s.i. More coal is required on the front, sides and over the tump in the continuous flap up, flap down routine, feeding the insatiable maw of the firehole.

We 'breasted the tape' at Brill, flat out along the falling gradient through Bicester, and then took the tunnel at Ardley at 50m.p.h.,— some speed for a train of this nature. We flew through Aynho and I gave the fire another good charge, for I must be ready for the water-troughs at King's Sutton.

With George keeping a sharp eye on the road ahead for the King's Sutton distant signal and the bell of the a.t.c., I then moved over on the right-hand side to operate the water scoop. From the inky blackness comes the white light to indicate the start of the troughs so down goes the scoop, all this while the engine is running flat out. It took only eight or nine seconds to collect some 4,000 gallons, which should take us to Rowington for our next pick-up. I had to keep a very wary eye on the tender gauge as we sped over the troughs, because a split second too long and we should be almost swimming on the footplate.

We were now racing towards Banbury and more coal was required, the great fire still one gigantic mass, ever-eager for more fuel. With the exhaust injector still working and pressure well up I was beginning to work well into the tender, as I continued to feed the apparently remorseless fire.

Banbury (South) is in darkness as we thunder through the station towards the north of the town where we are rising slightly towards Cropredy, which again showed clear. It was here that we passed one of our opposites working on the 'up' line to London, and gave him the 'Royal Salute' on the whistle of one long and one short blast, of which only engine crews know the correct implication!

Cropredy is now behind us, and the train virtually free wheels down the 14 mile falling gradient to Leamington. It is along this stretch that a breather can be taken, although the fire must still be kept well up for the task ahead.

In view of the speed and weight of the train, on this sort of gradient we had to have the earliest indications of the signals ahead, and this was greatly enhanced by the provision of the a.t.c. which, on many occasions, gave us an earlier indication than the visual signal. Ample distance was given for braking should we sight an adverse signal, and a case in point was the Fosse Road distant signal which was placed 1,000 yards out, while the ramp which operates the a.t.c., fixed in the centre of the track, is placed further out again.

We were now racing towards Southam Road and Harbury through a short tunnel, and we passed the distant signal for Fosse Road which was 'clear'. While on the subject of braking distances I have, on many occasions, heard enginemen state 'that it is not the running — it's the stopping' and believe me, it requires skill in no small degree to bring a fast train to a smooth stand from 60 or 70m.p.h. In the case of a passenger train one had to bear in mind, from the passenger's angle, that invariably when approaching a terminal station, many passengers are on their feet preparing to alight and to get luggage down off racks, and any injudicious brake application could cause passengers to be thrown off their feet, so any sharp application of the brake under normal circumstances must be avoided. The driver gets the 'feel' of the train by partial brake applications, before making the final one to bring the train to rest.

It would not be long before we sighted the distant signal for Leamington South, situated almost at the foot of the bank. Both Leamington South and North were clear so we prepared for the long bank up to Hatton. Through the dip at the north end of the station, we then found ourselves storming up the bank towards Warwick, the locomotive now being worked almost flat out with the regulator well over, the lever at 35 per cent and the engine exhaust a series of staccato barks as the great locomotive found her toughest assignment, Hatton Bank. Yet more coal and more flap — no peace as we thundered up the incline, this being where we required maximum power if we were to keep time, so I thought it opportune to give the fire a really good pull through with the long pricker, to ensure we were getting all the power possible. By now, with the tremendous amount of coal that had been consumed, the fire was showing signs of wear and tear with the mass of clinker that had formed on the grate area. We were now right in the middle of the bank with the engine functioning perfectly, but the water came in sight at the top of the gauge frame and I had to shut the exhaust injector off to keep the pressure up. Another good charge all over the box, with the clock now creeping up towards the mark, and we saw the distant signal for Hatton. Here George eased her down, and I quickly put the right-hand injector to work as the water was half-way down the glass.

With an easy stretch of road in front and almost to time, George put the regulator on to first valve which gave me a chance to get the boiler well up for the final burst through to our destination. With another flash round and with the blower on to induce more air through the grate I 'shaped myself', to quote George, for our final pick-up of water at Rowington which would take us to journey's end. We streaked over the trough, had another good flash round, and awaited the sighting of the distant signal for Lapworth where I gave the fire a good pull through with the poker; an instrument that required some delicate handling on a swaying footplate, and extreme care had to be taken when removing it from the fire as it was red hot. Believe me, it is some feat to handle this 12ft. piece of iron and manipulate it back on to the tender, without scorching the driver's trousers!

We were still forging ahead on the last lap of our journey, this being the easy stretch of line running right through to the outskirts of our native city. I was now working the fire down, with just a quick flash around to keep the pressure well up. It was just as well that the demand for coal had considerably lessened, as I was now working towards the back of the tender, and getting quite tired in the process. We then sped through Widney Manor, Solihull, Olton and

Acocks Green to catch the distant signal for Tyseley South, and we then prepared for our final burst through the tunnel into Birmingham (Snow Hill). As I explained in a previous chapter, Snow Hill Tunnel presented some rather unusual features with regards to working through, due to the gradient at its exit of 1 in 60. If 'line clear' was given then the passage through the tunnel was taken at speed to get through, so George gave her almost a full regulator at Bordesley South and we ran hard towards, and through the 'hole'. Despite this we were working really hard by the time we emerged into Snow Hill Station, with an exhaust fit to blow the chimney off. The station clock said 2.35a.m., and we had a minute to drop comfortably into our objective, Hockley, with the time at 2.36a.m.

The signals were off for the yard so we pulled our long train clear of the main line, and our thoughts were centred on a lovely can of tea which I considered we had both earned. Thus when we came to a stand, I stepped into the shunter's cabin to make a good brew. The examiners were now going round the train looking for any defects such as hot boxes and the like, and George was also looking around our 'steed' for anything unusual. I arrived back with the tea, which we promptly enjoyed.

While we were putting off the Carter Patison containers that we picked up at Paddington, the men employed by that company were waiting with their vehicles to carry them away within minutes of coming off the train. The two containers were under the crane, unloaded, loaded on road vehicles and away by around 3a.m., and the contents of these two containers would be delivered to their various destinations before 8a.m. that morning. Such was the standard of service in those far off days, and it is a matter of conjecture if such a standard is equalled today!

We stood clear while the yard shunter disposed of our train, and enjoyed a well-earned breather together with our 'char' and a bite to eat. Our task was not yet finished, however, as we had to take the 'shorts'; that is traffic for Wolverhampton and intermediate stations, to Handsworth, about half a mile up the bank. The time was now 4p.m., and we backed on to about twenty wagons and proceeded to Handsworth, where we backed inside and hooked off.

Our next move was to proceed to Birmingham (Snow Hill) and, on arrival at Birmingham North, we were turned into the yard and on to the turntable. The engine was then turned uphill that is, towards London, and we prepared the locomotive to work the first passenger train out of Snow Hill, which was actually the stopping train to London, timed to leave at 5.20p.m. I pulled the remaining coal forward, of which there was not too much left, and put the chisel bar

The author as an engine cleaner in 1921, alongside 4-4-0, No. 7 *Armstrong*.

A lasting reminder of the Great Western Railway, No. 7029 *Clun Castle*, fortunately saved from the scrapyard and preserved at Tyseley.

A view of the footplate of No. 7034 *Ince Castle* clearly showing 'the ever open door' or, in other words, the firehole to the firebox.

MIDLAND EXPRESS MISHAP.

DRIVING WHEEL BREAKS FROM ENGINE.

DRIVER'S PROMPTITUDE.

A mishap which might easily have had serious consequences occurred to the Dover-Birkenhead express when it was dashing through Olton at high speed on Saturday.

The express was due to arrive at Snow Hill at 3.10 and it was shortly before this that one of the driving wheels of the engine came off and rolled on to the bank at the side of the line.

The driver quickly realised that something was amiss and, acting with great promptitude, applied the brakes and brought the train to a standstill in a short distance, thus averting what might have been a disaster.

Wheel Down Embankment.

It was not until he got down from the footplate that the driver discovered what had happened. The leading near side driving wheel, one of six on the engine, had disappeared and the connecting rod was twisted. The wheel was eventually found some distance away on the embankment.

The express was full of passengers at the time, but they realised little of what had happened until some time later.

The mishap blocked the down main line traffic for some time. The express was held up for about an hour, the train being eventually hauled back to Solihull by another engine and thence to Birmingham. Here an express engine took it on its way.

Single line working was adopted while a breakdown gang attended to the disabled engine, a work that lasted some time.

Apart from the initial delay, the services were not greatly interfered with.

Newspaper cutting from the *Birmingham Post*, 3rd February 1930.

Above: 51XX class, 2-6-2T, No. 4178 an example of the 'Prairie' locomotive the author worked on North Warwickshire line passenger duties.

Below: No. 4031 *Queen Mary*, an early example of the 'Star' class. Note the brakes on the bogie wheels and the absence of top feeds on the safety-valve casing.

A view along Platform 7 at Birmingham (Snow Hill) in 1911, illustrating the 'important' clock.

Above: Members of the 'Motley Crew' at Tyseley in 1923, with No. 7 *Armstrong* prior to her rebuilding.

Below: Not Swindon built and the result of six years hard work, but a constant reminder of my days with the GWR.

Above: First in the long line of 'Castle' class locomotives, No. 4073, *Caerphilly Castle.* Designed by C.B. Collett in 1923 this engine gave long and useful service and was withdrawn in May 1960 after completing a mileage of 1,910,630.

Below: Saint Bartholomew – A remarkably easy runner and always a good steamer in the right hands. These qualities were reflected by the fact that 100 were built in the early years of the century.

Birmingham (Snow Hill), with platform 7 and the station clock in the background, as a North Warwick line train prepares to leave platform 5.

My son, David, and myself, pictured in unorthodox 'rear end' surroundings.

Above: The entrance to Snow Hill tunnel, Birmingham, at the end of platform 7. 'County' class, No. 6364 prepares to depart.

Below: No. 7820 standing on the 'run' at Oxley, near Wolverhampton. The 'run' was common to all sheds.

Above: No. 3440, *City of Truro*, pictured at Didcot — a very famous link with the past.

Below: The motive power of the 'Park Royal' — No. 4700, mixed traffic 2-8-0 locomotive.

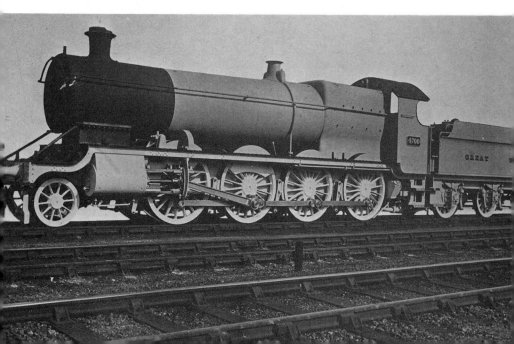

through the clinker in the grate; as our engine only worked the train to Leamington. It was now getting near train time and we backed on to our coaches, tried the vacuum, and proceeded to platform 7 to await train time. The guard came up to the engine and advised George, 'as per the regulations,' that we had six coaches for 180 tons, which was a mere bagatelle to what we had brought down from London.

At 5.20p.m. a whistle and a green flag meant we were away, but this time we would be relieved at Tyseley by a crew who were waiting for us there, allowing us to be relieved at 5.30p.m. A few brief words were exchanged and they proceeded on their way to Leamington, while we made our way down to Tyseley Shed to book off, which I did at 5.45p.m., having made seven minutes overtime! I was very ready for bed — having burnt, in the course of the trip, anything between three and four tons of coal in addition to the many duties associated with this particular train. May I say, in passing, that although this type of railway service entailed a considerable amount of hard work for me as a fireman and of course, a good deal of vigilance on the driver's part, it always had a fascination for me and was an experience I would not have missed. Before I end this chapter on fast timekeeping it is interesting to point out that although a good watch was essential for the driver to keep time, he was never supplied with that article and had to bring his own. Only the guard was provided with a Company watch, and I was always bemused as to why the men who kept the time were never supplied with a 'timepiece'. It is rather amusing and ironic that the only time a watch was supplied at the Company's expense was when retirement came!

My last trip with George was on a coal train, this being the 8.10 p.m. Sunday night Bordesley Junction to Banbury working with forty wagons of coal. Little did I know at the time of starting that we were about to part company, but during the trip something adverse happened to me which precluded any further heavy work, at least for some considerable time. As it was, I managed to work to Banbury with George taking a turn with the shovel and fortunately, on arrival at the 'hump' at Banbury, we were relieved and ordered by Control to return home 'on the cushions' to my intense relief. I booked off sick on arrival at Tyseley, and a visit to the doctor the same day revealed a rather severe hernia.

I was admitted to hospital for an operation, and the subsequent proceedings had rather an interesting sequel. I must have rambled rather a lot whilst coming round after the results of the anaesthetic, and the next day, the man in the next bed said to me 'You work on the railway son?' and in reply to my affirmative he said 'I thought so, you were working a train from London, and at a place called High Wycombe you were eight minutes down — whatever that means. This only goes to illustrate that the GWR was never really far from my mind and especially, at that time, the 'Park Royal'.

During my convalescence I was transferred, in my absence, to the Swindon link, and it was with the greatest regret that George and I parted company. We had spent a very interesting two years together and, despite his somewhat brusque manner, we had worked very well together as a team and I like to think that we invariably 'delivered the goods'. I was to miss his rather quaint philosophy, and also his sometimes very pungent remarks on human nature in general.

CHAPTER FIVE

Fred, Again

After a period of light work, I moved into the Swindon link where I rejoined my old mate of earlier firing days, Fred, with whom I had spent nearly five years on the 'pilots'. It was during this time that he had taught me many things to my advantage in the art of firing.

Fred was, as I have stated earlier, an outstanding character and a whole mine of information on a wide range of subjects, as well as being a singer and a very capable entertainer, he was also in great demand, as I have previously explained, as a narrator of rather dubious stories when we were assembled in the relief cabin, many of which would not bear repetition in the drawing room. He was also a great admirer of Robert Burns, and had quite a knowledge of that great man's observations on life and humanity in general. Many a time I have been treated to some of his special favourites on a moving train, one of which was Burns' 'To a Mouse' in which the poet describes an incident during the ploughing of a field when, upon turning over the nest of a mouse, he addresses the shrinking animal thus:

> 'Wee, sleekit, cowrin, tim'rous beastie,
> Oh what panics in they breastie!'

and concludes with the immortal lines:

> 'But Mousie thou art not alone
> in proving foresight may be vain
> the best laid schemes of mice and men
> gang oft agley.'

He would invariably quote this particular stanza when things had a tendency to go wrong. This was by no means the extent of his repertoire, as he knew by heart many of Burns' well-known works, and would quote as the occasion arose:

> 'If I'm your haughty Lordlings slave by nature law designed,
> why was an independent wish ere planted in my mind? or
> To catch Dame Fortune's golden smile
> Assiduously wait upon her
> and gather gear by every wile
> That's justified by honour.
> Not for to hide it in the hedge
> Nor for a train attendant
> But for the glorious priviledge of being independent'.

or one of Burns' greatest gems:

'Oh would some power the 'Giftie' gie us
To see ourselves as others see us
Two'ud from many a blunder free us
and foolish notion'.

It was this which Fred would quote on occasions when some individual 'got too big for his boots'.

I shared Fred's interest in the classics, but the difference was that I had a liking for Byron and Shakespeare, as well as Burns. Also one of my favourites was, and still is, 'Gray's Elegy', that immortal clasic that epitomises all the human foibles and yet runs to such extreme heights in his philosophy of the human race. One particular gem from the Elegy reads as follows:

'Full many a gem of sparkling ray serene
The dark unfathomed caves of ocean bear
Full many a flower is borne to blush unseen
and waste it's sweetness on the desert air'.

Also one of my firm favourites is 'Barbara Friechie', which is the story of the heroism of a very old lady 'bowed with her four score years and ten'. It is the reputedly true story of an incident between Stonewall Jackson, of the Confederate forces, and the little old lady and the flag of her country, the Stars and Stripes, in the American Civil War. Incidentally, this particular work was a great favourite of the late Sir Winston Churchill who was wont, on occasions, to recite it to his friends:

'Over the meadows rich with corn
Clear as a cool September morn'. . .

Another firm favourite of mine is 'Childe Harolds Pilgrimage', which includes 'The eve of Waterloo'.

'There was a sound of revelry by night
and bright the lamps shone on fair women
and brave men'.

Many passages from the work of Shakespeare have to me been life-long favourites although the best is, I think, the passage from 'Hamlet' concerning Polonious' advice to his son, Laertes:

'And these few precepts in thy memory.
Look thou character. Give thy thoughts no tongue
Nor any unproportioned thought his act.
Be thou familiar but by no means vulgar.
The friends thou hast and their adoption tried,
Grapple them to thy soul with hoops of steel;
But do not dull thy palm with entertainment
Of each new hatch'd, unfledg'd comrade. Beware
Of entrance to a quarrel; but being in,
Bear it that the opposer may beware of thee.
Give every man thy ear, but few thy voice,
Take each man's censure but reserve thy judgement.
Costly thy habbit as purce can buy.
But not expressed in fancy; rich, not gaudy;
For the apparel oft proclaims the man;
And they in France, of the best rank and station,
Are most select and generous, chief in that,
Neither a borrower nor a lender be;
For loan oft loses both itself and friend
And borrowing dulls the edge of husbandry.
This above all — to thine own self be true!
And it must follow as the night the day
Thou cans't not then be false to any man'.

There is another gem, this time from King Henry V, which takes me back to my schoolboy days when our master insisted we learn by heart King Henry's speech before Harfleur; Third Act, Scene 1.

'Once more to the breach dear friends once more
And close the wall up with our English dead
In peace there nothing so becomes a man
As modest stillness and humility . . .

We were now engaged on trains principally to Swindon with, of course, the inevitable 'double home' stint which we both viewed with dislike. It had the capacity to rob us of many creature comforts and, as I have previously explained, we often had to wait for someone to get up before we could go to bed for a much needed rest. Although these people who kept 'double home' lodges were, in the main, extremely kind folk, it was not like home but, of course, it was the old economic system of working on the part of the Company, and we therefore had to accept it. Gradually, this system was abolished and in exchange came well-appointed places where engine crews had much better accommodation, in institutions provided by the Company.

Our work in this particular link consisted of hauling mineral trains to Swindon. The 9.25p.m. Bordesley Junction train was a case in point, during which I well recall something that happened to upset Fred's usual equilibrium, and which he took considerable time to live down; he stopped the 'Cheltenham Flyer'! The 9.25p.m. ex-Bordesley Junction to Swindon working was usually made up to a full train of forty coal wagons and was, at that time, booked for examination at Toddington. It was the general rule to do a few chores while the 'tappers' were going round the train, and it was usual for us to top up the tank which would take us to Gloucester South Loop.

For some reason, which I am unable to explain, we did not take water, and only realised the fact when we were pulling away. However, we were both of the opinion that with careful working we should be able to make Gloucester for the water-column there, as it is a free wheel almost all the way. We did not take into account, however, that we had an injector that put more water on the ballast than in the boiler, with the result that with us just passing Cheltenham Racecourse Station, the injector flew off through an empty tender tank. This meant that Fred had no recourse but to stop at the water-column at Cheltenham (Malvern Road), and it was here that the fun began. I must here explain that the famous 'Cheltenham Flyer' started from Cheltenham (St. James), and we had stopped for water in a position that prevented the train from leaving. Of course, had the signalman known we were going to stop under the water-column he would have kept us at his home signal until the 'Cheltenham Flyer' had left St. James, but we were now in such a positiion with the water very low in the glass we just had to stop. Immediately we did, I nipped smartly up and pulled the column round, put the bag in and pulled the chain, this being one of those 'help yourself' water-columns with the fireman pulling the chain to operate the valve in the tank. It was then that we became aware that something was amiss, as the Stationmaster came up nearly having a heart attack and said we were preventing the 'Cheltenham Flyer' from leaving. We had forgotten this particular train in our anxiety to get to the water-column but, as it was, 'Flyer' or no 'Flyer', water we had to have. Whilst in the process of collecting this vital commodity we were forced to listen to the Stationmaster's comments which were not very complimentary, the results of which we were to hear in due course. I may explain here that had we possessed sufficient water in the boiler we could have pulled the train into the loop in which we were turned, and out of the path of the 'Cheltenham Flyer', but the water in the boiler was too low to risk any further movement. It was pointed out in the subsequent report of the Stationmaster that we could have pulled right into the loop to release the 'Cheltenham Flyer' but, as I have stated, the level was too low for pulling into the loop and would have meant taking water on Cheltenham Locomotive Shed, necessitating hooking off the train and risking any engine preventing us from taking water there. Thus Fred had the rather dubious distinction of stopping this world-famous train and, as I stated previously, it was some considerable time before he lived it down. A 'carpet' job for Fred followed reports of 'please explain', which he dealt with in his usual philisophically calm manner. Needless to say the grape-vine had been in action, and there were some pointed references respecting taking water when we entered the lodge at Swindon, and also when we returned to our home shed at Tyseley.

The 'Cheltenham Flyer' in those far off days was making railway history, and much has been written of the wonderful performances set up by the crews working this particular train. Many times have I viewed the passage of this train when we lesser fry have been inside, as a general rule, on the 'shelf' at Brimscombe, where we were shunted for her to pass.

Incidentally, in connection with the running of the 'Cheltenham Flyer', the signalman at Gloucester South has, on more than one occasion, let us go in front of the Flyer with just enough running time, forty minutes, to reach Brimscombe and back inside. Needless to say, it was one long belt in order to avoid repetition of the Cheltenham (Malvern Road) incident.

We had, as a general rule, some good locomotives on these trains, quite often a 28XX or a 43XX class, but sometimes an ex-R.O.D. was used, which very often required some ingenuity to keep on time and out of trouble.

It was with Fred that I received one of the greatest shocks of my footplate career, and one that remained with me for some time.

We were working the 9.50p.m. Birmingham to Swindon parcels train, an all-round trip of 206 miles, five nights in a week, which, due to the mileage payment at the time, was dubbed the 'Rent Payer'. It was a fast train calling at Cheltenham, Stroud and Swindon, with a non-stop return from Swindon due in Birmingham (Moor Street) at

4a.m. The locomotive was usually a 29XX or a 49XX class and, apart from the mileage, was a good comfortable job. The trip took us via Gloucester South, Stroud and through the Stroud Valley and up the bank, with Sapperton Tunnel at the summit. This was quite a climb, but well worth the time and effort from a scenic point of view as the Stroud Valley presents a really beautiful picture almost all the year round. After passing Sapperton we reach the easy stretch to Swindon, where we had a chance of a bite and a brew up, but not before taking water, pulling coal forward and generally preparing for the trip home. We have no need to turn the engine as our route now takes us through Didcot, Oxford and via Wolvercote Junction on to our West Midland line, which we leave at Honeybourne Junction to join the main line for Birmingham via Stratford-upon-Avon.

It was while working this train forward one night, round about midnight, that we were approaching Bishop's Cleeve with the distant signal off when, in the blackness of the night, we saw three red lights while doing between 60 and 70 m.p.h. Fred shouted something — which I was never able to comprehend while, at the same time, slamming the regulator shut with a full application of the brake. We then spent a few agonising seconds as we crouched in our respective corners, waiting for the crash. We were still running far too fast to jump off despite the application of the brake, — and we then sailed past a train on the opposite road! We later learned that the guard had failed to changed his tail and side lights after his train had been shunted on the opposite line for us to pass.

It is quite a normal procedure to shunt a train in this way to give precedence to a more important or faster train, but, of course, the signalman would not be allowed to return 'line clear' to the rear until the train had been run clear, and, the guard must exhibit his three red lights on his van until the whole of the train is clear over the points. The guard must then obscure his red sidelights and change his tail lamp to white, which the guard in question failed to do. By the time we had come to a stand, a very agitated and breathless guard came up, and was loud in his apologies and regrets. He was a Bordesley guard, and a very fine railwayman, whom we both knew very well but, in common with the rest of suffering humanity, was capable of making mistakes. However, with as little delay as possible — after we had recovered from the shock — Fred squared it with the signalman and the whole affair got no further, except for a rather sharp reminder on every trip we made through this particular section afterwards. Even to this day, nearly forty years afterwards, I can still vividly recall the few seconds before we passed the three red lights at Bishop's Cleeve, in the blackness of the night.

62

Almost every other week, we did three trips and back with our booked trains to our 'second home' one of which I recall became my toughest assignment. On these return trains, we were usually allocated either a 43XX or a 28XX class locomotive, or one of the engines returning to its depot after heavy repairs. On this occasion, though, we were allocated a locomotive that had seen the best of her days, No. 2408, a standard goods engine. The foreman said they wanted the engine back at Wolverhampton, and on the trip we came to the conclusion that she was to be put on the scrap-heap. Our train was the 10p.m. stores working, a regular runner which was loaded to the engine's capacity, and it was a real struggle all the way with the engine suffering many 'blow ups' in the section. This train was routed home via Didcot, Oxford and the West Midlands through Wolvercote Junction and after leaving there, some very long blocks are enountered. Fred said 'We'll go inside at Campden and have a go at the fire!' We were fighting a losing battle and our friend, the Swindon parcels train, was waiting at Wolvercote for us to clear and reverse into Campden. The distant signal here was visible from a very long way out and, with the pressure falling and the water in the glass getting lower and lower, Campden still seemed a very long way away. Very thankfully, we reached Campden and the signalman by now had only got his feet in the box and was shouting 'Back inside, the parcels is waiting'. He needn't have bothered, as we were going inside in any case. Back inside, and Fred gave the three short whistles indicating we are inside the loop points, and I set to work to get the clinker off the bars, as the rest of the trip home is not without some really difficult gradients.

The signals were now off for the Swindon parcels train and as they passed us, we were informed in no uncertain terms their sentiments at having been stopped. We were given the 'Royal Salute' which, as I explained previously, has only one meaning to an engine crew. Had we had a decent engine we should have been back inside for them at Campden, and we could well understand their feelings on the matter, as no one working a mileage train gets any benefit from being late, with the loss of overtime.

With the parcels train out of the way, the loop signal was pulled off for us and we resumed the struggle to Tyseley, losing quite a lot of time on the way and not without a few 'blow ups' in the section. The Shed Master had received notice of our performance and stopped the engine for lengthy repairs, thus ending a really heart-breaking trip which defied all our joint efforts to keep time. There are occasions when one's ingenuity is taxed to the utmost when, for no apparent reason, the engine will not steam and this was one of them, but we did eventually get home.

Another train in our link merits more than a passing mention, this being the 4.22p.m. Gwinear Road to Bordesley 'C' headmarks. We were booked to run from Westbury (Wiltshire) to Acocks Green in Birmingham non stop, a journey of 136 miles, but before this, we booked in at midnight for a rest at Swindon, before travelling down to Westbury to take over. Once there we walked over to the engine, now taking water and with the fireman busy bringing coal forward, to offer our assistance, with the knowledge that once we were away there would be little time to walk into the tender after coal. We also had to bear in mind the fact that the engine had already run a considerable mileage, and the small residue of coal left something to be desired.

After a few shunting adjustments, our guard declared 'forty five number threes Fred', appertaining to our limit on the train. Our train this time was comprised entirely of GWR oil boxes, this being a good sign as we frequently got 'foreign' wagons on the train with vacuum leaks galore, which the vacuum pump, worked off the piston crosshead, failed to overcome. The result was that the small ejector had to be used, thereby making further demands on the boiler, and the fireman.

At last we were able to leave Westbury with everything under control, and I was pleased to see that the fireman had left me a really good fire, which I gave a good pull round as the engine got into her stride and headed for Wootton Bassett and Swindon. We had a good mount in the 49XX 'Hall' class, a locomotive quite capable of dealing with a train of this description and timing. Indeed, this particular class was so successful that no fewer than 400 were built in the 49XX, 59XX, 69XX classes, as well as the modified 79XX. No matter what the train, be it express passenger, express freight or a heavy coal train, this particular class was a delight to work.

We passed Wootton Bassett Junction on our way to the home of the Great Western Railway, Swindon, about which many tomes have been written which extol the products of that great locomotive engineering centre, and the great names associated with the works. However, as we shot through Swindon Station the works were in darkness as it was the small hours and, apart from the sound of our 'steed', peaceful and quiet. A few hours later and the whole centre would be one great hive of activity, turning out everything appertaining to railway operation, including locomotives.

We left Swindon and raced towards Foxhall Junction, Didcot, where we eased down for the restriction at the junction. Our next passing point was Oxford (North Road) and the regulations and time allowed us five minutes at the water-column if we had a 3,500 gallon tank. If we possessed a greater capacity 4,000 gallon tender tank we were given instructions to run through, but Fred said 'we'll box clever here and stop for water, and something else' meaning a good brew up. We stopped at the water-column at Oxford and put the water bag in the tender tank, pulling coal forward, with one eye on the billy can that was now almost boiling. At this point Fred was having a quick look round and oiling the cups over the pistons, and feeling here and there for anything unduly warm. Thus in just five minutes we had coal forward, tank full and, just as important, a brew up of very much needed 'char' after our long run from Westbury. Many times we experienced this five minutes together at Oxford, (North Road) but if we exceeded the time limit there would be a report to answer. We did this frequently in all weathers including rain, snow and fog until I often wondered if there was any future in the job, but I was always sustained by Fred's philosophy and encouragement. Good old Fred would always take a hand with the shovel, and as I knew the road equally as well, the change was very welcome.

A smart getaway saw us getting well into our stride, with the fire well up and pressure on the mark, as we approached Aynho Junction where we joined the main line for Banbury and beyond. We then took water at King's Sutton, enough to take us to Rowington and our final destination of Banbury. We then passed Cropredy and screamed down the bank through to Leamington with a clear run up the bank to Hatton, all the time feeding the fire and keeping the boiler well up. At last we were on the home stretch and soon sighted the distant signal for Acocks Green, and we prepared for our relief. We then stopped at the home signal and our relief stepped aboard, allowing us to wend our way down the shed and eventually home, where the first thing I was interested in was 'up the wooden hills' for a much needed sleep.

Our jobs were very interesting, and we had the satisfaction of a job well done and on time, but they were very exacting and took their toll. It is, therefore, small wonder that the initial medical examination was so very stringent and meticulous.

World War II was, at that time, very near, and preparations were in hand for a mass exodus of schoolchildren to safe areas. A huge programme was arranged, and the ordinary timetable for passengers was suspended while this was underway. I remember the scenes at all stations in and around Birmingham when thousands of our children and their teachers were entrained; my daughter being among them. She, together with the school, were taken to Lydney in Gloucestershire where, in common with the majority of evacuees, good people had been found to take them in.

It was on Saturday, 2nd September 1939 that I made my last trip with Fred, and this was not without incident. We were booked on a special in connection with the impending hostilities, and were relieved at Oxford with orders to return home 'on the cushions', and we congratulated ourselves on our good fortune. It was, however, getting rather late and we took what I believe was the last 'stopper' which terminated at Banbury, — the time now being approximately 10p.m. Our next connection was the stopping train standing in the bay and in complete darkness, as a directive had been issued to that effect. We were advised by the station staff that the stopping train in the bay would follow the fast train as per usual arrangements, so we put our 'traps' in this train and proceeded to the refreshment room for a little sustenance. It was then that we heard the rumble of movement outside, and Fred said 'that's the fast — we had better get out now to catch our boat'. When we got outside, we were informed that due to the fast train being exceptionally late, the 'stopper' had gone first — together with our boxes, hats and coats, and we were left more or less high and not quite dry at Banbury. However, we telephoned Leamington to make clear our situation, and due to very capable staff, our belongings were taken off and placed on the seat where we could locate them in the dark, and so we had no option but to wait for the express to take us to Leamington, where we eventually landed at 1a.m. Sunday morning. After recovering our belongings we advised control of our situation and these gentleman, after a few pungent remarks, made arrangements for a 'down' freight to be stopped to pick us up and drop us at Tyseley. We finally arrived there at 7a.m. on the morning of 3rd September, having been away from home about 24 hours. On that fateful day, War had been declared and I terminated my association with Fred as a fireman. I did this with infinite regret because although I was extremely fortunate in all the men I was called upon to work with, Fred was outstanding in the very many excellent qualities he possessed. Amongst these qualities were his courage, his love of the classics, his poetry and his philosophy, the latter covering any contingency in his and our lives. Of course I did not lose sight of Fred, and was able to observe his progress through to his early retirement, and to the time when he passed on. In short, he was a truly remarkable person, who left a lasting impression on my life.

CHAPTER SIX

Hostilities

At noon on 3rd September 1939 our Prime Minister, at the time Mr Neville Chamberlain, announced that we were at war with Germany and I, in common with untold millions of others, found my path in life totally different from that which I had envisaged. Possibly a platitude, but how many of us have any idea of what is in store for us in this life of ours, and how many of us can truthfully say that life turned out just as we planned? This is a claim very few can make and, in point of fact, someone once said 'the future is mercifully hid from our eyes, and it is just left to mankind only to hope'.

This day also marked another milestone with regard to promotion as I was now in the top freight link, — the Birkenhead jobs, — running principally to Cardiff and Bristol. Also, I had a new partner in Frank, — a very dedicated engineman and an extremely good mate with whom I was to witness some very peculiar incidents, not specifically quoted in the book of rules.

It was at this time that I decided to visit my daughter who had been sent to Lydney, which was considered a safe area. Special leave was absolutely out of the question so I arranged to change turns for the week with a fireman on the Gloucester run. On this particular job the engine crew went in for rest at Cheltenham, and this would give me an opportunity to visit my daughter at Lydney during the period when we were booked off. Thus with the consent of the office I exchanged turns, and booked on duty during the Monday night for the 1.20a.m. Bordesley Junction to Gloucester trip. The driver happened to be a very old friend of mine and a man well respected in the community, and although not exactly a martinet he was a man who liked, and indeed insisted upon, a job being performed properly (or else). However, by reason of the fact that I now had considerable experience in every class of work at the station, I could view with equanimity any driver with whom I was called upon to work.

The locomotive was always prepared by another crew due to the lengthy time engaged on the trip, and we took over No. 5156, — a rather unusual locomotive for this particular job. This was because the regular engine was not available, due to the general disorganised state of engine working following the outbreak of hostilities. We had a full cargo from Bordesley Junction with the usual 'belt' through the tunnel and a stop at Hockley for reforming our next stop, the 'stop board' at Rowley Regis. This was a compulsory stop for all goods and mineral trains, under the Company's rules governing train working down inclines.

I must mention here, that these instructions were very necessary in order to work trains down steep gradients, as at the time about which I write, very few trains were vacuum-braked throughout. The procedure was as follows: the train is brought to a stand at the 'stop board' and when the starter, — that is the signal, — is pulled off, the train is slowly pulled on to the incline while the guard pins down the wagon brakes. He continues to do this until the driver is satisfied that sufficient brakes are applied to steady the train down the 1 in 60 incline. He then gives two short sharp whistles from the engine and the guard rejoins his van, and I exchange signals with him using the gauge lamp. This item is always carried, and used at night to exchange signals with the guard, to exhibit a red light in an emergency and, the main purpose, to illuminate the water gauge glass. We then, on this particular instance, proceeded down the incline and quickly discovered that the wagon brakes were not holding. As our brake was held in reserve along with the guard's brake I then applied my brake to bring the train under control, but nothing happened. Bill, my temporary mate, could see I had put my brake on and we both realised that in addition to the train brakes not holding, the engine handbrake had developed a serious defect and that repeated applications of the vacuum-brake also brought about no reduction of speed. We had now entered the tunnel at Old Hill with the train gathering speed and were practically running wild. We passed Old Hill signal box with the brake whistle blowing flat out while asking the guard for more assistance with his brake. I yelled to the bobby that we were out of control although, in any case, it was hardly necessary to do so because we passed his box at a phenomenal speed for a goods train. We were now hurtling down the bank almost helpless to do anything about retarding the speed of the train and, as a last resort to lessen the speed — which, by now, was really alarming, — Bill put the engine into reverse. This had the effect of converting the cylinders into pumps and although the action may bring about a retarding effect, air is forced into the boiler to such an extent as to cause a heavy discharge of live steam from the safety-valves. There is also a great risk of damaging the valve gear. William then tried a small opening of the regulator, but this only tended to lock the wheels and so had to be abandoned. Our only hope now was that we could get round the rather severe curve in the section ahead, — there being one consoling thought in that I knew that the section ahead and that Cradley East and Cradley West would, or should, be clear of any obstruction in front. This was because these two boxes were not allowed to return 'line clear' to Rowley Regis and Old Hill unless their sections were clear. There were, as I mentioned previously special precautions concerning incline working which were designed to deal with just such a situation as we found ourselves in but, believe me, — despite this knowledge, — we were both feeling extremely uncomfortable as we belted down the bank, helpless to do anything but hang on tightly and hope for the best. We finally came to a stand at Lye signal box, about a mile from Stourbridge. On examining the brake gear we found the main brake shaft had fractured, rendering any brake application on the locomotive completely impossible. The signalman at Lye advised Stourbridge Locomotive Shed of the circumstances, and a fresh locomotive was prepared for us to work forward from Stourbridge. William has since passed on, but I can still vividly remember, even after such a passage of time, our experience down Old Hill Incline, on the occasion of a visit to my daughter.

We were now in the first few months of the 'Phoney War', a period of the hostilities when nothing seemed to be happening, and many of our children came back under the impression that the mass exodus of the previous September was unnecessary. How wrong we were was soon to be proved in the very near future.

The air was now full of directives regarding the precautions to be taken by railway staff in general and, of course, we footplatemen had the full measure of instructions covering all possible contingencies due to the war and enemy action. Footplatemen had a particularly difficult job in preventing any light being observed from the air, and the measures taken to obviate this could be rather trying as we were, literally, working in a sort of tent, with the fireman lifting the flap up every time he went to the tender. If one required to look-out of the side of the cab he had to negotiate a contraption which was virtually a spring-loaded curtain, and the aforementioned flap had the capacity to precipitate a stream of water down one's neck in wet weather, and if anything was blowing or leaking and causing condensation, it would be like working in a turkish bath.

To add to our difficulty with regards to look-out, the eyeglasses were partly painted with a special paint, which was supposed to turn a certain colour in the event of a poison gas attack, and in connection with this we were issued with special respirators and steel helmets. When one presented himself for duty, he looked more like a frontline soldier than a 'common or garden' railwayman.

There was also a special book of rules and regulations governing the working of trains during the war, and specifically for working during enemy air raids. During the early months of the outbreak of hostilities it was considered necessary to curtail almost all movement, even if hostile aircraft were many miles away, but due to the dislocation this caused, a new system was introduced. Under this scheme, the country was split up into regions and depending on the position of enemy aircraft, a system of colour warnings was used. Purple meant that aircraft were crossing the coast but work could be carried on, and it was not until aircraft were imminent that we were put on the red warning, indication of which was given by the sounding of very powerful sirens giving an undulating note. It was then that all activity stopped, until the sirens sounded a long note indicating all clear. This system was used by the majority of our great national concerns including factories, exchanges and many other organisations concerned with war effort. There was to come a time in the not too distant future when, due to the nightly and almost continual visits of the raiders, the majority of folk remained at their jobs wherever they were, and only went to the special sheters when ordered to do so, and when it became too dangerous for them to remain at their posts. Such was the indomitable spirit of the people on the 'Home Front', to produce the much needed materials for the smooth running of the British effort.

Very stringent instructions were issued with regard to trains working during air raids. If there were enemy aircraft overhead we were stopped and advised by the signalman that a red warning was in operation, although this was often a superfluous observation when we could see and hear the bombs falling, and could frequently see the showers of incendiary bombs in the immediate vicinity. If the signalman was able to get the line clear ahead then we got going 'pronto', especially if our train was carrying bombs or ammunition. Under the instructions in force we proceeded at 4m.p.h. while trusting to luck that the road ahead was intact, as these raids were always made at night, rendering it impossible to see the state of the track. In this vein, I well remember a 72XX coming to grief in a crater made by a direct hit on the track. On one occasion we were working the Swindon parcels train and after the booked stop at Cheltenham, the signalman advised us that the region was on the red, due to a very heavy raid on the city of Bristol. We proceeded at 10m.p.h. after I had altered the headlamps, as per instructions, to only one in the middle, as an indication to signal boxes in front that we had been warned. In the far distance we could see the flashes of bombs and gunfire, as well as the explosions of shells in the night sky, but as we passed Gloucester South box all hell broke loose. A battery of guns had opened up nearby and shortly afterwards, we could hear the shrapnel beating down on the cab roof. It was for Frank and I a baptism of fire because as yet, the Midlands and Birmingham had not been under attack. Frank shouted 'What do we do, should we keep going? to which I replied 'Keep going, let's get out of this' so we hastened towards Swindon, with the guns at South Cerney blazing away in the distance. It was at Bristol that Frank and I saw our first really severe air raid. We were approaching Stapleton Road when we saw the barrage ballons go up, — a sure sign of trouble, — and fortunately we had the road into Bristol and arrived on the shed at St. Philip's Marsh just as it was getting dark. We booked off and hurried to our lodge at Totterdown just as the sirens were sounding their ominous note of warning, and there we found that due to previous bomb damage the gas supply was non-existent, so we could not have the usual fry up and cup of 'char'. More urgent events soon claimed our attention in the form of intense enemy action and, for the greater part of two hours, Bristol was under seige. Never before had we seen damage sustained like this and neither had we witnessed the showers of incendiary bombs that rained down and set fires going all over the city. As well as this, the noise of the bombs and gunfire was simply appalling. We had the all clear at about 10p.m., and retired to bed hoping for a decent rest, only to be disturbed by further alarms, but we stayed put and reported for duty early the following morning. This then, was to become a familiar experience for the next few months, with us booking in for rest at Bristol every other week by which time we, in common with many, were getting more or less used to the nightly visits of the raiders. In connection with these activities I recall vividly being held at Westerleigh, just outside Bristol, while a particularly savage raid was in progress. The evening in question involved a very clear sky with a full moon by which a newspaper could almost be read, and the raiders seemed to be right over our heads as they made their run towards Bristol. We must have stood out in sharp perspective to the enemy, but no attempt was made on the train.

We move on to June 1940 when events in France were beginning to assume very serious proportions for our troops, culminating in the unforgettable glory of Dunkirk. My diary at that time, dated 2nd June 1940, records that on that day, Sunday, I booked on duty as usual at 1.35a.m. for the 2.55a.m. Bordesley Junction to Bristol 'double home' service. Upon arrival in Bristol I would book off at 1.35p.m., returning after rest to work the 11.20p.m. Stoke Gifford to Bordesley Junction train, after which I booked off at our home station, Tyseley, at 7.20a.m. Monday. With barely twelve hours off we booked on at 8.05p.m. Monday for the 9.50p.m. Birmingham to Swindon parcels train, a 209 mile long journey. We did this same trip on five nights that week, clocking up a total of 1,045 miles for the five round trips, eventually booking off on Saturday at 5a.m. That same night, we booked on again at 9.45p.m. on a special Bordesley to Snow Hill banker, and booked off duty at 7.40a.m. the next day. The major part of seventy hours work, involving 1,000 miles, was rewarded the following pay-day by the princely sum of £9 4s. 1d. This was not bad going for those days, but it also illustrates the tremendous differences in payment for a similar performance at current rates of pay. To us it was a small fortune, but earned only as a result of excessive hours and mileage.

The following week I was, according to the roster, 9a.m. spare, which meant I could be booked on any job with the fireman away. Thus I was deputed to work the 9.10a.m. Birmingham to Cardiff passenger service, returning the same day after a journey of 246 miles. I was booked to work on this train on alternate days of that week, while other days were spent with the Birmingham pilot; an engine specially kept at Snow Hill to cover any emergencies. During that particular week I worked a further 1,000 miles for which I received £5 17s. 4d. — not exactly a small fortune but, as emoluments went in those days, it was quite good and very acceptable.

Each succeeding week saw more booked visits to our second homes of Swindon and Bristol, with workings to the latter being adversely affected by enemy bombings on the city. It was on Tuesday, 13th August that my diary for 1940 recorded that Birmingham had its first taste of war and so began, in common with most of our larger cities, the ordeal of intense fire and bombing from the air. Fortunately I was at home that night and was able to look after my wife and family, but it was with some misgivings that I viewed the immediate future when my duties took me away for lengthy periods. Gone was the prospect of coming home and getting a night's sleep after a Bristol trip, as we were now to experience enemy action at both ends of the trip, until after a rather bad night at Bristol after working forward the 10.15p.m. Oxley Sidings to Bristol train, for which we had booked on at 12.20a.m. on Tuesday morning, and we were in for rest at Bristol at 5.50p.m. after seventeen hours of continuous duty. The following morning, we received orders to work back the previous night's 9.15p.m. vacuum train to Wolverhampton, which had been delayed by the usual raid. All our food had been consumed on the forward trip due to the long hours, so we had to draw on the very meagre rations supplied by the shed, and so we booked on duty at St. Philip's Marsh after nine hours off, and while things were fairly quiet, we slipped away hoping that we should get a good run home. Alas, despite our hopes and plans, we were stopped everywhere between Bristol and Gloucester, and when we finally reached Gloucester signal box, the signalman had us turned towards the South Wales road. This was the last straw, as we had now been on duty for more than twelve hours with absolutely nothing to eat between us, so Frank dug his heels in and went to the box and informed the controller of our position, and that we were not prepared to work the train further. These, of course, were very strong measures to take, but we were getting desperate, with no hope of getting away for hours due to traffic in front. The controller had many problems of course, with the allocation of relief men being stretched to the limit, but he appreciated our position knowing the time we had left Bristol, and although he had no relief for us, he bent the rules by sending a cleaner out to look after the engine until he could get a crew to work the train forward. So we were safely shunted back into Gloucester Yard, and could leave the engine to our cleaner friend, and as the time by now was 3p.m. our immediate concern was something to eat. The station foreman said that the next train to Birmingham would be the 4.40p.m. LMS working and we had ample time for a wash, after which we obtained all we required at a nearby cafe, and both of us felt better disposed to the world in general. It is said that a 'hungry man is an angry man' and believe me, when we saw that the train was turned in the direction away from home, we really felt like 'nothing on earth'.

However, the inner man was now satisfied, and we waited in a better frame of mind for the passenger train to take us home. We left Gloucester at around 5p.m. and, after an uneventful journey, just as we were approaching Birmingham (Selly Oak) and congratulating ourselves that we would soon be home, the sirens were heard. The train then stopped and proceeded under the regulations which I have previously described, and as we entered Birmingham (New Street) the raid began in earnest. I said to Frank 'If we hurry we can make the 7.15 stopper' — and we both made a bold dash across the city to Snow Hill, only to find that the 7.15 was still standing at platform 7, and was not likely to depart for some considerable time due to a fire that was now raging at the other end of the tunnel. The raid had now assumed very serious proportions and we, in common with many hundreds of would-be passengers, were ordered to go down the subways underneath the station, and so began another period of frustration, but things were too warm outside and all we could do was 'bide our time' and wait, hoping that those at home were safe. Towards midnight the raid petered out, but due to the tremendous conflagration which was out of control at the other end of the tunnel, no traffic was allowed through.

In the company of several other railwaymen we walked through the city to Moor Street passenger station, where a train had been formed to get as many people home as possible. We eventually booked off at around 1a.m. Thursday morning, having been away 48 hours instead of the usual 24, and out of the 48 hours we had completed two spells of duty of about seventeen hours each. In point of fact, at the time of booking off, we were actually due on duty for our next trip. All semblance of ordered working was thrown out of gear, and it became very obvious that a reorganisation of timing of engine crews had to be made to cope with the chaos arising out of the delays and disruption caused by enemy action. Men were frequently coming off duty when they were due on for the next turn, and because of this the management decided to temporarily suspend 'double home' working. This was much to our relief, as we now had more time at home with our families and could endure whatever was in store. This was just as well, because the raids became worse and lasted much longer.

My own house was damaged, and finally, in November 1940, I decided to take my family away to the small market town of Henley-in-Arden, about twelve miles from the city, where some kindly folk agreed to take them in. Here, they would be 'more or less' spared the ordeal of persistent nightly raids, while I soldiered on at home and fended for myself. It was just as well that they were out of the way as Birmingham was now experiencing some really intense air raids — culminating in the great raid on Coventry. I was a witness to this event, being off duty at the time, and also in connection with my duties as Air Raid Warden; a task which I performed with the limited time at my disposal.

Whilst it is outside the scope of this book to enlarge on the effects of enemy action and the attitude of people in general, I think it worthwhile recording the tremendous courage shown by almost everyone, and their indomitable fortitude to carry on and live and work under such appalling conditions. People became closer to one another in their desire for company and solace, although, possibly, it was a comradeship born of fear. Often have I envisaged this fellowship to be of a lasting nature — but this was possibly wishful thinking.

Frank and I parted company in 1941, after some very hectic turns of duty which had involved one or two 'close shaves', and it was with Fred that I did my last few months as a fireman on the goods or express freight workings. As 'double home' work was now cancelled, we had a system whereby, at a given point on the route, we changed over with a train that we should normally have worked back home, had we been on 'double home' runs, and as there was very little enemy air activity, we were able to work almost to time, and exchange with our opposite number at Shrewsbury and work back home.

In June 1941 I was appointed Passenger Fireman after an examination of rules and regulations, together with a working knowledge of the mechanism of the locomotive. This meant that I was now qualified to take charge of a locomotive and work locally, and it made quite a welcome change, even though the occasional duties were only confined to engine preparation, and the odd shunting job. My time with the shovel was nearing its end, as I had completed seventeen years with that implement.

I was now in the Passenger No. 2 Link and my mate was William, a product of the 'old school' and a man steeped in the best traditions of the Great Western Railway. Indeed, he was every inch a good railwayman who liked things to be done right, and in the old locomotive jargon, he was 'particular' in every respect, while being clean almost to the point of fastidiousness. The water gauge glass merited his 'particular' attention, and he was quoted as saying 'I want to see the water as well as you, mate' to a fireman with a glass not properly cleaned, and the water level only visible to the fireman.

William was a brilliant engineman, with the knowledge to exploit to advantage the expansive qualities of live steam which meant, of course, that he would watch the lever very carefully and this frequently resulted in us performing many stretches with the lever almost in mid-gear. With the Welsh coal we used, the fireman had to be extremely careful in his method of feeding the fire, as the exhaust would obviously be very light, and under these conditions the fire could very quickly become blocked. What William would have said if the fireman needed to use the 'poker', I could only imagine.

I worked with William for the next six months, and it was a treat, as we had our own engine or, to be precise, we shared this particular locomotive with only one other crew. After the trials and tribulations of preparing 'common user' engines, where we often had to spend our preparation time looking for essential tools, it was wonderful to step on to the footplate with the knowledge that everything would be to hand and securely locked up. This, of course, being a reciprocal arrangement.

William made one observation on our first day together which illustrated his keenness but, to me, at the time, was rather niggling. By this time I had accumulated seventeen years firing experience, I was also a passenger fireman and approaching my 40th birthday, but having been warned of his pet aversions, which included indiscriminate blowing off at the safety-valves, I was not surprised at his remarks: 'Harry — these jobs can be gauged to a shovel of coal and a bucketful of water'! Although it was putting rather a fine point on the job, it was certainly true. As I have previously stated, the proper control of a boiler, in terms of steam pressure, showed the hallmark of a good fireman. William has since passed on, but I remember with extreme pleasure our time together, short though it was, and the meticulous standards which he observed. He was representative of the best traditions of the old Great Western Railway, and shared, in common with the great majority of locomotivemen, a deep and abiding dedication to that organisation which, to our lasting regret, is no more — the Great Western Railway.

My next, and last, mate was Ralph of Wrexham who I have already mentioned. Ralph and I were together for only a few months, but despite the wartime conditions under which we were working, they were very pleasant indeed

In April 1942 the great day arrived when I was again to enter the portals of Park House, Swindon, the place of so many hopes and fears. This occasion was my examination for promotion to engineman, and in due course I was ushered into the presence of the great man himself, the Locomotive Examiner. He was a somewhat austere but kindly man who, no doubt, had been through all this in his time, as every aspirant to footplate work has to do. Under the Great Western Railway, all locomotive supervisory staff were recruited from the footplate, in other words, enginemen only, and the Locomotive Examiner must have had a rough idea of how I was feeling. He motioned me to a seat and, with his back to me and looking out of the window he proceeded to put me through my paces. He asked questions on rules and regulations, more rules on this and that and 'What would you do with this and that'. 'What action would you take in this instance' and so on. Single line and double line working were more or less covered and the fact that I had the GWR certificate of general railway operation stood me in good stead, and appeared to satisfy him. Next came a detailed examination on the general mechanism of the steam locomotive, with its faults, failures — and the remedy. At the end of the ordeal he turned round and, to my intense relief, said 'OK Son, the best of luck' and he then shook my hand. Many men must have passed through his hands in the course of his career as an examiner, and I felt at the time that he carried rather a lot of responsibility with regard to the future conduct of those to whom he had given the OK. Not all the men who appeared before him were successful — at least, not the first time.

If a man failed he was sent back to think it over for three months and, when that time expired, was given another chance. In this connection I well recall a fireman being asked the question 'What would you do if you found, on entering a dead end bay, you were unable to stop with a passenger train?' This question was designed to test the candidate's knowledge of vacuum-brake regulations. Back came the prompt reply from the would-be-driver, 'Oh, I should pole her' meaning he would reverse the engine and apply steam. This, by any standards, was most reprehensible and dangerous, as the wheels would quickly pick up and considerable damage could be done to the locomotive valve gear. He was promptly sent back for three months to find a better, or correct, method of procedure. The question was fair, as it is extremely necessary to observe the correct procedure when entering a dead end with a passenger train. It is a well-known fact that a passenger train is brought to a stand under normal circumstances by the application of this vacuum-brake on the train, but in the case of a passenger train being turned into a bay the stop should be made by the handbrake operated by the fireman, and the speed of the train regulated by the driver before entering the bay. The vacuum-brake is actually held in reserve should the fireman be unable to stop the train before the stop blocks are reached. These regulations were in force at the time about which I am writing, and possibly do not bear any relation to present day practice. However, our friend fared better the next time he went to Swindon and this time he was able to satisfy the examiner that he knew most of the answers and I know, from my own personal knowledge, that he turned out a very good and capable engineman.

So in April 1942 I passed out, not without a few qualms, to the 'right-hand side' and knew, as I had known a long time, that 'drivers do not wear halos', and have a very responsible job to perform.

The war had now reached a very critical period and much reorganisation was in the air, and to cope with the ever increasing burden on the railways many new supervisory posts were set up. In response to an appeal by the Management I volunteered and, after an interview with the District Superintendent, I was selected for one of the posts. It was only after very careful consideration that I took this step, having regard to the fact that I had reached my goal of being an engineman, — with the opportunity of realising my ambition, to do a spot of locomotive driving while in charge.

But, on second thoughts, it was a temporary measure and at most, only for the duration of the war, My new duties were diametrically opposed to anything I had done previously, as I had been shovelling coal for the past eighteen years and now, suddenly, I was drafted, as it were, into a completely new life. I had more or less 'gone over the fence' and although my many friends still appeared amicable on the surface there was, I could sense, an air of restraint which caused me a little concern. To illustrate a point, it became very embarrassing for me to have to give, or transmit, orders to men I had been associated with all my working railway life, especially men of the 'old brigade'. However, in the main, I got on fairly well in my new environment and found the work extremely interesting, involving, as it did, a lot of responsibility and necessitating the frequent making of split second decisions, the results of which could be far reaching if one made a mistake or made an incorrect assessment of a particular situation. I certainly gained an insight into the hourly problems confronting the relief controller, whose duties consisted of providing relief for train crews working over our particular region. These men had very often been on duty for long hours, and it was the controller's responsibily to get them home when the train they were working was held up in a siding, and had little chance of moving for hours.

On frequent occasions I have been in the same boat, and quite often felt rather angry when advised by the relief controller that he had no men to spare at that moment for our relief. It went down very hard to accept the position, especially when we had been away from home for a lengthy period, with all our food gone and no prospect of moving. I could now 'see the other side' and appreciated the difficulties of the controller trying to make the best use of the men at his disposal, in the light of the tremendous disruption of timetables due to the demands of the war effort. However, in the main, the spirit of the main body of men was very good because they accepted the situation and worked loyally under almost intolerable conditions; they were ambassadors of GWR standards.

Locomotives of all sorts and conditions were worked, and often taken off the shed with fires not being cleaned after preparation in almost total blackout as, of course, no outside lights were allowed. In short, every train crew carried on under totally foreign conditions, to the usual Great Western Railway standards and 'delivered the goods'.

At Tyseley, we now had a very mixed bag of locomotives to augment our own dwindling allocation. Swindon was, at this time, turning out war material and consequently engine repairs were held up to a large extent. To replace engines out of commission the GWR took possession of some fifty engines from the London & North Eastern Railway, of which Tyseley received about five. They were promptly named 'Graf Spees', after the German battleship which had sunk some time previously in the River Plate battle. These locomotives were not unlike our Standard goods 0-6-0 engines in appearance, but there the likeness ended. They had had their day, and I believe they were actually on the condemned list before being rejuvenated for service on the GWR. Everything on them was strange to us, and to get water into the boiler the fireman turned certain valves and offered up a prayer, in addition to giving the clack box several discreet taps with the coal pick.

Working through the stretch of line which included the rush through the tunnel and up the severe incline into Snow Hill Station, taxed the resources of any driver, while the fireman had his work cut out maintaining a good head of steam. A further disadvantage was the locomotive's tendency to 'prime' if the water showed more than half a glass, and this was a frequent cause of coming to a dead stand in the tunnel, with consequent serious delay to following traffic. No doubt, in the dim and distant past, these locomotives had been some Northern enginemen's pride and joy but now, to us, they were 'anything but'. Still, it was only for the duration of the war, and engine crews took them off the shed and hoped for the best.

Our stock of locomotives was now augmented by a batch of new engines from America, and weird contraptions they appeared to us on first sight. Despite this they quickly proved their worth, although it was extremely difficult for our men to get accustomed to something so totally different in design. These new locomotives had a tractive effort equal to our 28XX engines, with a similar wheel arrangement of 2-8-0, but there the similarity ended. It was not prudent to mount the cab in the dark unless one had previous experience in the daylight, as everything to us was where it shouldn't be. The water gauge frame was pitched extremely high on the boiler back plate and, in consequence, we, who always worked with the water level well above the gauge, found that a similar practice with the American engines caused flooding of the boiler which, in turn, prevented the regulator from closing correctly. The result was that on more than one occasion, the said engines tended to run out of control.

I recall that when assisting in charge on the shed, one of our crews brought such an engine to the depot with a very strong complaint that the engine could only be reversed with great difficulty, and with the aid of a long tube on the reversing lever for greater leverage. We stopped the engine for examination and found that, in our opinion, no lubricating oil was reaching the cylinders and piston valves. The Americans had an arrangement whereby it was possible to examine the valve heads by the removal of two 4in. plugs which, when removed, exposed the working surface and also the piston valve rings. The engine was 'set' with the big end in a certain position at top or bottom centre with the lever in mid-gear and in this position, with the plug taken out, it could be ascertained if the rubbing surfaces were being properly lubricated. In this particular case the heads of the valves were a rusty red and with the very small tolerances allowed between rubbing surfaces, it was remarkable that the driver was able to move the reversing lever at all. In my opinion, no oil had reached the valves since she left America! However, when our boys got used to these engines and their particular peculiarities, much good work was performed by them until they were withdrawn at the termination of hostilities.

My supervisory duties frequently took me to Birmingham (Snow Hill) Station, where I deputised for the regular Inspector on leave, or sick. It was the duty of the aforesaid Locomotive Inspector to cover any emergencies arising, and to generally supervise the working of locomotives in and out of the station. In view of the very many arrivals and departures, the job was no sinecure.

Should an engine fail for any particular reason, it was my job to provide power 'on the spot' to cover the failure with the minimum delay, as trains were leaving Snow Hill, 'up' and 'down', every few minutes. I may explain that all locomotives had a specific job to perform, usually termed diagram working, or set working and, due to this, one had to be very careful when interfering with a particular engine's set working. A case in point, if the 3.05p.m. local train engine fails then we had no alternative but to commandeer the engine which was waiting in the siding to work the 4.10p.m. service. The 3.05p.m. engine out of commission, was due back into Snow Hill to work the 5.10p.m. train to Wolverhampton. Thus the 4.10p.m. working was now short of power which had to be covered by another locomotive and so the position snowballed, until resources were stretched to the utmost to keep the traffic moving, and to keep delays down to a minimum. Believe me the job could, at times, be a real headache when trying to sort things out.

What memories the name Snow Hill conjures up for me, and it is with intense regret that I view what is now left of the once proud station that represented all the finest traditions of the GWR. I recall the long platforms that were always clean and well-kept, its maze of signals and track and the general ordered expectancy of this arriving, or that departing. I remember, too, the massive station clock on platform 7, reputed to be the meeting place of countless thousands over the years and where many a tryst had been made and kept under its massive face. So many times have I watched, when time and circumstance allowed, the comings and goings, the fond meetings and the many sad partings. The newly-weds, full of hope and joy, with a retinue of well-wishers — the carriage doors sometimes bearings comments such as 'just married', 'keep out', etc.

I have frequently seen the capacity of this once great station stretched to the limits of its boundaries, while the press of passengers waiting to go on holiday has been so great, with people standing right up to the edge of the platform, that we have had to almost inch our way up the long platform to avoid an accident where passengers were standing too near the locomotive. This was when famous trains like the 'Penzance' ran in no fewer than seven parts to get folks to their several destinations and this major operation provided a very hectic time for station staff and the locomotive department but, as a general rule, everyone got away. This was, of course, before the more general use of the motor car, and it is open to question, in view of the extremely congested state of our roads and the frustration caused by long delays, if the journey by rail is not more preferable to the ordeal by road. I am glad to say that the 'Penzance' is still with us but has been renamed the 'Cornishman', and instead of the once familiar 'Castle' class, with its flamboyant air of speed and power, we have the not so spectacular, but equally powerful, diesel locomotives.

Memories of my wartime experiences, while acting as Locomotive Inspector at Snow Hill, come flooding back. These include many thousands of armed forces men who were seeing this country for the first time, mainly Canadians and Americans. I also recall thousands of our own boys on their way to duties abroad, complete with the trappings of war. Upon seeing these men I was reminded of the time, two years previously, when I had been the fireman working trains which conveyed our boys straight from the beaches of Dunkirk, the majority of whom had only the uniform in which they were standing. In spite of this, their bearing was truly great in view of the terrible ordeal they had undergone, and I now saw them returning for what promised to be the 'turning of the tide'. Snow Hill at this time and, indeed, at almost every hour of the day or night, saw every sort of serviceman and many the sorrowful parting I have unwillingly witnessed when so many were torn from their loved ones. In compensation, I have also seen very many happy reunions of men and their folk. Many ex-servicemen will no doubt remember the man who looked after their interests at all principal stations, this being the R.T.O. (Railway Transport Officer). He was also a soldier, and numerous and varied were the stories he was told by serving men who had missed their train. Alas, today, the great building is no more, and never again will it echo to the sound of mighty steam and surging crowds; these scenes now only existing in the memory of those who knew it well.

Gone, also, is the great locomotive shed at Tyseley, just a little way up the line, which was the one-time scene of so much industry when railways were in their heyday with the rush and bustle of engines leaving the shed every few minutes. It was a work of art on Monday mornings to get every locomotive off the shed on time, and an extremely difficult task for the crews in charge of the turntables when as many as perhaps five or six engines were booked off the shed at the same time. This went on for two or three hours every Monday, after locomotives had been off duty on the shed for the weekend. Both passenger side and goods side turntables were continually swinging round as various engines became due for departure, and this was a regular feature on every morning of the week when at least fifty or sixty locomotives were turned out for service. Although Tyseley has lost its status as a great locomotive shed, it is extremely pleasing to know that 'live steam' still lives there, due to a very dedicated band of railway enthusiasts. These people have formed an organisation to keep alive the interest in steam locomotives, chief amongst which is the very fine *Clun Castle*, restored to all her former glory. This wonderful locomotive, together with various others, attracts many thousands of enthusiasts at intervals on the open days, and amply demonstrates, in no uncertain manner, that steam traction still commands an enormous amount of interest from all quarters.

We were now in the early months of 1944 and, due to various personal reasons, I decided to resume my normal driving duties. A situation had emerged which brought me at variance with the local management regarding a growing tendency among the latter entrants to disregard the essential foundations of service, or, in other words, discipline. I had been raised, in common with my contemporaries, in the old GWR tradition, and found it rather difficult to accept the attitude and behaviour of these younger men although, in fairness to them, they were not railwaymen by choice. In fact, they had been directed on to the railways by certain Government regulations and, to be quite fair to these boys, many of them would have preferred the forces but, at that time, they were too young. Consequently, their heart was not in the job, and as a direct result, many cases arose of continual absence from duty, lateness and a general disinclination to do the job in hand — this at a time of extreme critical condition regarding the war effort. Due to these continual upheavals, it became increasingly difficult to maintain schedules and, finally, a particularly bad case of a young fireman's insubordination which, in my opinin, merited punishment, was passed over by the local management. Thus I could only register my protest by resigning from supervisory duties. I hasten to add, that these incidents were not typical of the majority of our crews, who went about their duties in the true spirit of the old Great Western Railway and carried on under some very trying conditions, some of which have been previously described.

I was now back on the footplate doing local work, and an occasional passenger job, when one night, a night to remember, I was performing engine preparation duties on 5th June when, in the very early hours, we all became aware of considerable activity in the air. Upon going outside the shed we could see a procession of aircraft heading south; this being the start of the Normandy invasion and the turning point in the conflict of war. When I arose at tea-time, before going on night duty, I learned that the invasion was well under way in the greatest military, naval and air action in recorded history, the date being 6th June 1944.

A few weeks later the blow fell, as far as I was concerned, in that something happened which altered the whole course of my railway career and, in due course, I found myself pursuing a path which I had never before envisaged. The first indication that something had gone wrong was on Monday, when I was fortunately booked on the shed to 'foreman's orders' — a position to cover any emergencies. I duly booked on duty at 3a.m., but on my way to the shed I felt a very sharp pain in my right foot which became progressively worse with every step. By the time I reached the shed, I was more or less incapable of further movement. Fortunately I was not required and towards the end of the shift I booked off, and was taken to hospital. There an X-ray examination revealed an unusual type of fracture and, as a result, my right leg was encased in a plaster cast from the toes to the kneecap. This remained so for the next sixteen weeks, during which time, of course, I was off duty. However, I was able to get around with the aid of a steel stirrup, which was incorporated in the plaster cast. Towards the end of the year I was discharged from hospital and, under the right foot, I was wearing an appliance prescribed by the hospital surgeon to prevent any further injury and also for support.

When I next reported for duty I was sent to Swindon for a medical examination, which was the usual procedure after an accident or illness. So, once more I entered the portals of Park House, Swindon, where the Company's Medical Officer pronounced me fit for light duties only, and that meant no main line duties. There was nothing for it but to accept the situation, as he was the sole arbiter of my fate and there was no appeal. He suggested, however, that my case could come up for review at a later date and, with that pronouncement, I had to be conent and so, for the moment at least, all my main line aspiriations were set at nought. The great consolation was that I should still be associated with my early love, the steam locomotive, and in this connection little did any railwayman dream, at the time, that the great days of the steam locomotive were drawing to a close.

The GWR Directors maintained an extremely magnanimous view with regard to men like myself who were removed from the line of promotion by the degree of the Medical Officer at Swindon, and every effort was made to find steam work suitable to such a man's condition. During my time, many men failed the very stringent eyesight test, which was compulsory, on the GWR, at intervals of five years of a man's working life. Any engineman or fireman failing this test was always found work commensurate with this particular defect. The step down usually carried with it a reduction of 1s. 0d. a day but, in my own case, I was not on top rate so it did not seriously affect me moneywise. Later on, all men who had been removed through defective eyesight, or for other medical reasons, received the same rate of pay that they would have received had they been on normal duties; a most generous gesture on the part of the Company.

At the beginning of 1945 I was transferred to Small Heath, also known as Bordesley Junction, where I was employed as a shunting engineman. The junction, situated about a mile from the main Tyseley Shed, was a huge concentration yard with six, and sometimes seven, engines working round the clock, seven days a week. It was here that traffic from the north, south, east and west, and several thousands of goods vehicles of every description were dealt with every day and night. Indeed, it could rightly be described as the 'hub' of the industrial Midlands. The majority of trains terminated here and in turn were formed into other trains, depending on the route for which a particular wagon, or wagons, were destined. Many times in days past have I started from here with trains for Swindon, London, Cardiff, Bristol and, indeed, all points on the Great Western Railway system. Now I found myself exployed, no less usefully I trust, in the reverse position of forming these trains instead of working them away. The locomotives employed here were, in the main, the 57XX and 36XX 0-6-0 engines, and were quite comfortable for the job in hand.

Bordesley Junction was also the starting point for newly-appointed firemen and, of course, it was our duty to ensure that they knew the rudiments of proper manipulation of the fire and the boiler. It can be assumed that much patience was required to teach the novice how to put the coal on 'the right side up', the correct manipulation of the shovel, the level of water in the boiler and so forth but, bearing in mind my early days, I was able to appreciate their anxiety when their efforts met with little success. At the same time, of course, I had to keep a sharp eye on the shunters working the engines back and forwards in response to their signals.

As previously explained, at this time men were still being directed on to the railways under a Government Order and, in consequence, we had the usual type who did not take too readily to this particular job and the irregular hours. One boy who tried my patience sorely, in particular, springs to mind. He was quite a good lad at heart, but without the sightest idea of the duties of a fireman. His previous occupation was completely opposed to his present duties, and keeping the footplate clean and tidy was to him an unnecessry task. He had, however, other qualities which I had sometimes to curb, as when he was perched on the top of the tank taking water and I would be regaled with a selection of arias from some well-known operas. Although the vocal performance was good, the folk in bed at that time would not have appreciated it. At one particular point in the yard the water-column was situated very near to many houses, and on some occasions we would require to take on water at 3a.m., so, of course, the fireman's vocal efforts were not conducive to sleep.

These boys were with us until they attained the age of eighteen, by which time they were required to join the forces. Due to this, and having regard to this boy's apparent inability to keep things really clean, I would remind him, in a paternal sort of way, that once in the forces he would have to do things very differently indeed. I said to him, on occasions when he was remiss in keeping the footplate clean, 'One of these days you will be in the Army' and he would, at once, with a very sheepish grin, apply himself to rectifying the omission. He eventually left me to go into the Army and, on his first short leave he came to see me, almost with tears in his eyes, and said 'Harry, you were right — what do you think? — the Sergeant threatened to put me on a charge for not cleaning the tongues of my boots'. It was, for him, a shattering experience. I doubt if previously he had ever, at any time, used polish on the outside, let alone the tongues. I am very pleased to record, however, that one of my later mates, who went into the forces, met my 'erstwhile non-polisher of tongues' while serving with the occupation forces in Hamburg, and he told me that he had turned out to be a really smart and very efficient soldier. I never saw him again, but it proves, of course, that many excellent qualites are latent within the mass of mankind — sometimes only to be revealed under compulsion as in the forces. I like to think that I may have been, in some small way, instrumental in directing his undoubted capabilities into better channels.

The war eventually came to an end, and I settled down to accept the inevitable course of events. The job had its advantages, shift work it is true, but unlike the freight train working, involving irregular and uncertain hours, we knew just what time to expect our relief which invariably came on time.

A wide variety of young men passed through my hands on their way up the ladder, and Lou was a case in point. On Monday morning we had to proceed to Tyseley Locomotive Shed to prepare our engine before operating at the junction, which meant that Lou, who lived some considerable distance away, had to rise very early to be on duty at 4a.m. This involved a cycle ride through very dark country lanes in the still small hours, and he would sometimes confide in me that it was, in his own words 'rather spooky', and that he felt very nervous. This young mate of mine left railway service some time afterwards to join the police force, and I met him on several occasions in the course of his duties. Later, he was awarded the Queen's Medal for bravery, after disarming a dangerous character who was brandishing a loaded revolver — no mean feat for the young man who, a little earlier in life, thought the country lanes were rather spooky!

Ken came to me straight from serving in the forces. A native of Cardiff, he was transferred to us on promotion to fireman and was an outstanding character, with a very fine military record for a young man, and excellent qualities which soon assured him a wide circle of friends. Ken's first few days with me showed that he was extremely anxious to do the job properly, but in common with all new entrants, he quickly discovered that 'coal heaving' could be almost an exact science. On several occasions a surreptitious look at his worried face as he viewed the falling pressure gauge, and the water level likewise, despite his attempts to maintain the boiler told me he was in difficulty. The trouble was that he was firing too heavy and too often, and with soft Welsh coal this could soon lead to trouble, as I had found by making the same mistakes in my youth. Soft coal can only be fired little and often, and only in places where the fire is burning well. It was just a matter of coal on coal and so, to avoid him further embarrassment, I sent him for a billycan of tea, to the canteen on the other side of the road. As soon as his back was turned it was a simple job to get the 'poker' and give the fire a real good root up, with the result that, by the time Ken returned the pressure guage was almost on the mark and with the injector working, water was well up the glass and his astonishment knew no bounds. It was then that I explained to him where he had gone wrong.

It was a procedure that always worked as I found it best for the fireman to make these mistakes and for me to later point out where things had gone wrong. In the main I like to think that these elementary instructions stood them in good stead in the later years on the more exacting work of the main line. I was rather particular in liking things well done, even if only on a shunting engine. Never, I trust, was I a martinet although I have been called an 'old woman' behind my back, but I always believed that 'anything worth doing was worth doing well' and also that 'the man that never made a mistake never made anything!' I only intended to instil into these young men that special atmosphere of good service which would be beneficial to them to maintain the best traditions of the Great Western Railway. Ken eventually left on promotion to Tyseley for main line work, and was transferred to Cardiff where he later left the service. We corresponded for many years, and have never actually lost touch, even to the present day.

By this time I had become the mens' representative of the Local Departmental Committee, this being the office set up at all locomotive depots under the provisions of the negotiating machinery at that time. Each depot had its own representatives whose function it was to meet the Management at stated times, to discuss any matter arising in respect of the working or conduct of their particular shed or area. Quite democratic in form, the Management met the men in a 'round-table' conference to iron out any difficulties or discuss requests for improved working and so forth. Sometimes it was the men who put forward suggestions for improvements in the very involved work of railway operations or, on other occasions, it could be the turn of the Management. In the event of disagreement, these matters went to the higher authority of the Sectional Council who, in common with the Local Departmental Committee, worked within the framework of the National Agreement and for many years, this system worked very well indeed. This was a far cry from the old days when, if one had a grievance, he was subjected to the tender mercies of an officious and unsympathetic individual, into whose presence you walked with 'cap in hand'. I recall with great pleasure the extremely cordial relations that existed at all times in our meetings with the Management.

I was to be the mens' representative for the next seventeen years, being re-elected every three years during that time, and the experience was extremely interesting in view of the many changes that took place, including a complete reappraisal of the whole railway system, its methods and procedures. Above all, it provided a measure of consolation for the post I had always aspired to and failed to realise, although, in any case, the writing was on the wall for steam traction. Had I reached my objective it would have been short-lived, as future events proved with the introduction of diesel traction. In 1948, to quote the words of a famous statesman 'The Wind of Change' came in the form of nationalisation, and, for all GWR men, the end of an era.

CHAPTER SEVEN

The End of an Era

The image of the Great Western Railway was slowly being obscured, and replacing the old spirit and enthusiasm was a system that was completely foreign to us proud 'Westerners'. Many of us, to our intense surprise, ultimately came under the influence of what was to us a 'foreign' region, and although I do not refer to that region in any way disparagingly, it was with great difficulty that we envisaged ourselves belonging to the London Midland Region of British Railways, after serving all our lives with an organisation we held in high regard — the Great Western Railway.

We were, in time, to become subservient to a totally different method of working and procedure, as the old traditions and all it meant in association with the famous name of the Great Western Railway had disappeared for ever. Gone also were the administrative set-ups — swept away and replaced by systems we hardly understood. In the Northern Division of the Great Western Railway our chief, the Divisional Superintendent, was the higher authority and only answerable to Swindon on matters of high policy, he being directly responsible for the whole of his particular division, including all matters affecting disciplinary procedure. He was now relegated to a secondary position, being directly under the surveillance of the Division Traffic Superintendent. This was completely alien to us, as it was a step unheard of in the Great Western Railway. Large chunks were eventually taken over and incorporated into the London Midland Region and, of course, the personnel of all grades became members of that group. When, in due course, I received my Valedictory Certificate on retirement, it was with extreme regret that I noted that it was given by the LMR instead of the Great Western Railway. Was I being too sentimental on this point? Traditions and ideals die hard!

Under nationalisation the railways came under the control and management of the British Transport Commission who, of course, were now responsible for the conduct and procedure of the four great groups. Consequently, during the next few years, many changes were introduced concerning operational methods and personnel. It became increasingly obvious that due to various causes, the railways were losing ground financially. The falling revenue was due, in the main, to continually increasing competition from road transport concerns, and also to the burden of capital charges arising out of the takeover change due to nationalisation.

Another factor in the demise of railways was the growth in numbers of private motor cars and the building of new motorways, all contributing to falling revenue on the railways.

In 1959 the Government of the day issued a White Paper dealing with the modernisation plans. The provisions of these plans were far reaching, and involved numerous startling changes, but it is outside the scope of this book to comment on this, and certainly not within my province to condemn or condone. The specific aim of the plan was to bring the railways up to date in the light of modern progress, and the greatest blow, so far as we steam locomotivemen were concerned, was yet to fall — this being the total abolition of steam locomotives in the not too distant future. We were soon to see a complete reorganisation of services running under a new system of traction — diesel and diesel-electric locomotives. Steam locomotives became less and less in number until, finally, the last steam locomotive was withdrawn from service in 1968.

The picture of rows of these once proud steeds of ours, waiting their turn for the breakers' yard was a very sad spectacle, indeed. Up and down the country the scene was the same, and literally thousands of locomotives were put on one side waiting to be towed into oblivion. On numerous occasions and, possibly, in a nostalgic mood, I viewed these one-time wonderful giants of power and speed in all their pristine glory but, there it was, progress!

However, the greatest consolation to me, is the tremendous enthusiasm for preserving quite a considerable number of these fine locomotives, sometimes right out of the breakers' yard. This gives an indication of the ever growing interest and keenness to keep steam alive. One only has to visit an open day at one of the places where steam locomotives are now housed, to appreciate the extent of this interest, and I place on record the enormous amount of hard work and devoted service these men have contributed in their efforts to care for and put into working order some of the finest examples of British locomotive design. We most not forget, however, the smaller editions that have also been rescued, at a price, from the scrap heap.

CHAPTER EIGHT

The Abolition of Steam etc.

It was round about the early 1950s that we were advised of proposed changes in locomotive working at our particular depot at Small Heath and Bordesley Junction. The entire steam power allocation was to be withdrawn and replaced by diesel-electric shunting locomotives, which were being built in ever-growing numbers by outside contractors. Subsequently, a directive was issued by the Management that these machines were to be put into operation at the earliest possible moment. The difficulty was that, at that precise time, no such locomotives were available at our depot for instructional purposes, and as the nearest depot was Washwood Heath, a large yard on the London Midland Region, arrangements were made for a number of men to attend a five day 'crash' course. As the mens' representative I formed one of a small party of four and we duly travelled to Washwood Heath for our introduction to diesel-electric traction. There we learned how to drive these machines, being extremely impressed by their performance and the ease with which fifty loaded wagons of coal were hauled up a rather stiff incline. With regard to the inner working, the mechanism and what made these things tick, I have to admit we hadn't a clue!

The following Monday I met the Management, two Inspectors and the Chief Diesel Inspector from Swindon. The latter was a gentleman with whom I was to be very closely associated during the next few years, in connection with the continued development of diesel locomotives operating at our depot. He was one of nature's gentlemen, and a man I came to admire greatly. It was, very largely, due to him, that I was able to acquire the necessary knowledge to impart instruction to others who eventually passed through my hands.

William could be described as the father of Western dieselisation, as he was responsible for the initial stages of introduction of the newer form of traction and, in consequence, carried a considerable amount of responsibility on his shoulders. Nevertheless, he was always ready and willing to listen, and to the very many requests he had for information which were put to him each time we met, which was usually once every Monday.

There was one particular occasion when we were discussing the ways and means of putting these new locomotives into service; the only man knowing all the answers regarding the mechanism being William, as I had only the very vaguest idea of how they worked. In the event, I volunteered to take the first diesel-electric locomotive off shed while Ernie, one of the Swindon Inspectors, was to ride with me on the following morning; this being Tuesday. The locomotive I was to work stood outside, and we boarded her for a demonstration run. All concerned were satisfied that I could handle the machine, after several operations of moving various dead steam locomotives, and the Inspector was surprised at the ease with which very heavy loads were moved. The locomotive was duly rostered to leave the shed at 5.45a.m. the following morning for service at Bordesley Junction but Ernie, the Swindon Inspector who was to ride with me, now posed a problem. Ernie, a man whom I had known for many years during the time he was an engineman at Tyseley, and who was now based at Swindon, said that he would like to visit a relation of his at Wolverhampton, and 'would I care to take the new machine off shed without him, as it would not be possible to get to Tyseley in the morning and he would join me during the next day to see how I was progressing'. In any case, regulations stated that no locomotive was allowed to leave the shed for main line work without a second man, so I informed him that providing I could have my regular fireman I would do as he requessted, so this was arranged. I was pleased to get my own mate, as he was a very good boy indeed, who would be equal to carry out any instructions, assuming we inadvertently came to a stand on the main line on our way to the shunting yard.

Tuesday morning eventually arrived and I reported for duty at Tyseley Locomotive Depot at 5a.m., together with my regular mate. There diesel locomotive No. 12070 stood just outside the sheds waiting for the encounter, and there was a small crowd of sightseers who were viewing for the first time one of the new diesel-electric locomotives. The majority were my own footplate colleagues together with some shed staff — some of whom had come to cheer, and some to offer 'ribald' comments concerning the new form of traction.

The duties of preparing these new locomotives were completely foreign to that of a steam locomotive, but certain elementary duties were possible with my minimum of previous instruction. These duties I carried out in front of what I thought to be an admiring crowd, and it was not until I attempted to start the diesel engine, and failed after several attempts, that my audience, in a somewhat facetious manner, suggested various remedies, including a tow. I had forgotten one very important operation, without which it was virtually impossible to start a diesel engine, and that was the closing of two long switches situated on each side of the locomotive. These I

92

now remembered, so I climbed down from the cab and closed them — the crowd accepting this as part of the regular procedure, as I was being careful to conceal the fact that I had inadvertently made this important omission. The engine now responded to my further attempts with a lusty roar, and I considered we could now attempt the passage, and very gingerly we moved away to the cheers and jibes from the concourse. The date was 1st May 1951. I was perforce to work for the rest of my railway career with a medium I had never envisaged and, at that moment, I did not have the remotest idea of how it worked.

The dream of my boyhood had long since vanished and, in any case, steam was now on its way out, even more quickly than the planners had proposed. Therefore I had to devote my interests to the new field of railway traction and, as events proved, it was rather ironic that I, who held the steam locomotive in high regard, should be the medium to impart the elementary functions of the diesel-electric locomotive to many of my fellow locomotivemen.

The new locomotives were now being delivered in ever increasing numbers and I, as the mens' representative, was requested by the Management to start a pilot scheme whereby men could undergo a short period of training. It was almost a case of the 'blind leading the blind'. I was released indefinitely from my driving duties, and built up a system of, more or less, the elementary principles of diesel-electric traction to enable men to take charge and deal with simple failures. Being of a rather enquiring mind, I decided to glean as much information as I possibly could from the only textbook available on the subject, in conjunction with the very excellent teaching of William. It was he who, during weekly visits, always imparted some very useful information, or gave the answers to many aspects that bothered me at the time. I was now in a better position to pass on instructional matter, thanks to him, and due to intensive study I believe I gained a clearer picture of what happened 'under the bonnet'.

Men were now coming to me, for what instruction I was able to give, from many depots on the Western Region, including Banbury, Leamington, Stourbridge, Wolverhampton, Shrewsbury and, of course, from my own depot and Tyseley. In the main these were enginemen removed from main line duties due to various causes including failing eyesight, sickness and accident, and all were performing shunting duties. Another factor was that all these men were getting on as regards age and, obviously, a man who has spent the whole of his working life in steam did not take too easily to the newer form of traction. Bearing this in mind, a simple form of instruction with a subsequent examination was devised, commensurate with the safety factor and the initial cost of these machines.

This became an extremely interesting and absorbing experience, and I met all sorts of men who, I like to believe, appreciated my efforts on their behalf. Of course, it can be rightly assumed that many times when we had a short respite from instruction, the conversation would invariably veer round to the days of yore and steam locomotion, and many and varied were the accounts of each incident.

After a while and, I might add, due to the help given by William, I acquired a fairly extensive knowledge of the diesel-electric locomotive, and its many features which, at one time were completely foreign. Bearing in mind the many enginemen who still had to receive instruction I decided, not without much careful thought, to write a small work which would present the essential features in a more or less elementary way, in order that the older man, in particular, would be able to understand them. For the better part of twelve months I worked on the script, together with numerous drawings and diagrams. I was extremely fortunate in obtaining permission to do this from our Chief Running & Maintenance Officer, C. R. L. Rice, Esq., his kindness and encouragement standing me in good stead. But, without William and his knowledge, the book would not have been possible.

The British Transport Commission were supplied with a draft for consideration to be given for official publication, unfortunately, due to various reasons, it was not accepted but, at the same time, however, I received good wishes from higher authorities should I decide to publish. So after much correspondence with people responsible for building these new locomotives, and obtaining the OK for this and that, I approached a publisher, Wilding & Son of Shrewsbury, who agreed to publish my book *The Diesel Electric Shunting Locomotive*. In due course this book was published and made available to anyone and, in due course, ran into a second edition.

The greatest recompense gained with regard to the publication was the very many letters received from all over the United Kingdom from men who, like myself, had to forsake steam traction for the diesel-electric locomotive.

CHAPTER NINE

David

In addition to the very many kindnesses extended to me by Mr Rice, one which gave my youngest son, David, the thrill of a lifetime was a trip on the 'Pines Express' during the last three weeks that this particular train was worked by a steam locomotive — this being only a few weeks after my retirement in 1963. Permission had, of course, to be granted and, in addition, a Locomotive Inspector had to accompany my son. While we were waiting on platform 7 at Birmingham (Snow Hill) a very interesting conversation took place between David, myself and Locomotive Inspector Jones, with whom I was closely associated during my diesel training days. The 'chat' was tape recorded together with the subsequent sounds of the actual trip — to this day, this remains one of David's most valued possessions. This was an experience that many young enthusiasts would have given much to have made and, for the record, the locomotive was No. 7019 *Fowey Castle.*

As the years passed by, so my life with the railway came to a close, but I carried into my retirement very many memories, some of them happy, some of them not so, but it is always with pride and affection I remember, above all, my days and associations with the old Great Western Railway.

Of the future, who can tell? The forward thinking designers are now envisaging fantastic speeds in the foreseeable future while, at the time of writing, the 150m.p.h. Advanced Passenger Train is becoming a commercial proposition. It is not for me to philosophise on these new efforts or to waste space on the advisability of doing so, as I would rather remember, at the risk of being called old-fashioned, the marvellous and speedy performances of steam locomotion. May I reiterate, that the ever growing interest in the considerable number of steam locomotives preserved and working is a great source of consolation to me, and to my contemporaries, who regarded the 'Iron Horse' with the greatest affection and esteem — with special reference to the Great Western Railway.